BITS of Bargello

Karen Gibbs

Located in Paducah, Kentucky, the American Quilter's Society (AQS) is dedicated to promoting the accomplishments of today's quilters. Through its publications and events, AQS strives to honor today's quiltmakers and their work and to inspire future creativity and innovation in quiltmaking.

American Quilter's Society

P. O. Box 3290 • Paducah, KY 42002-3290
www.AmericanQuilter.com

Attention Photocopying Service: Please note the following--publisher and author give permission to photocopy pages 16–17, 28–29, 48–49, 65, 81 for personal use only.

Additional copies of this book may be ordered from the American Quilter's Society, PO Box 3290, Paducah, KY 42002-3290, or online at www.AmericanQuilter.com.

Text © 2009, Author, Karen Gibbs
Artwork © 2009 American Quilter's Society

Executive Book Editor: Andi Milam Reynolds
Senior Editor: Linda Baxter Lasco
Graphic Design: Lynda Smith
Cover Design: Michael Buckingham
Photography: Charles R. Lynch

Library of Congress Cataloging-in-Publication Data

Gibbs, Karen, 1966-
  Bits of bargello / by Karen Gibbs.
     p. cm.
  ISBN 978-1-57432-983-4
  1. Patchwork--Patterns. 2. Strip quilting. 3. Art quilts.
I. Title.
  TT835.G5275 2009
  746.46'041--dc22
                               2009008067

Acknowledgments

There are so many quilters who were involved in the process of creating this book. I am so thankful to belong to a wonderful, supportive quilt guild, Wings Falls, and be able to take quilt retreats with these crazy quilters.

Thank you to all my sample makers—Sally, Gail, Peg, and Carol—who never rolled their eyes at the whacky ideas. Thank you to the enthusiastic "guinea pigs" who took bargello classes at the studio and kept coming back for more! And of course, Marge, who can put a binding on anything.

I also want to thank the local quilt shop owners who mix my palette for me, assuring me that, yes, Jinny Beyer's fabric does blend well with Kaffe Fassett (Jim and Bob); bargello does work with reproductions (Shannon); and thank you Barb and Vicki for the retro baseball!

Thank you Casey, Justin, Marlous, and Mary Ann for your advice and humor that kept me motivated to continue searching.

And without the unbelievable patience of Andi and Linda, through two ice storms, this book wouldn't have been written.

And of course, thank you to my precious little ones—Jack, Madison, and Olivia—who inspire me every day and convince me to look at the world through their eyes.

Thank you Khai, for encouraging me to pursue my passion and making sure I always have books on tape to keep me going.

Contents

Introduction

Bargello became my focus almost as soon as I learned about quilting. I was new to quilting and making an all-bargello quilt is something of a rite of passage for a quilter. I made one. I even went so far as to quilt it by hand with metallic thread! I loved the idea of it but hated the endless matching of seams.

Bargello has been around for a long time—in textiles, needlepoint, upholstery, and, of course, in quilts. It's a traditional design in most of these mediums with the exception of quilting! Usually in textiles the bargello motif, the flame or the ogee shape, is repeated over and over to get the desired effect. Quilting takes this concept to a whole new level!

Rather than creating a quilt that is entirely bargello, *Bits of Bargello* utilizes bargello as a design element within a quilt in three different ways: bargello in landscape, bargello in blocks, and bargello as reverse appliqué. The essence is to restrict the bargello to specific areas of the quilt, placing it where it is most effective, then repeating it again and again across the quilt.

Bargello in landscape creates the illusion of movement. It can mimic the shading variations in nature. The bargello can be manipulated to fit into whatever shape you like. LET'S PLAY BALL! and ADIRONDACK WINDOWS use bargello in landscape designs.

Bargello in blocks achieves dramatic results by strategically replacing certain parts of a block with bargello. It's a way to play with color, add movement, and spice up a traditional pattern by changing its look. MOONSTONE FLOWER and BARGELLO LONESTAR are examples of this technique.

Bargello as reverse appliqué adds the illusion of movement, depth, and sometimes even a three-dimensional effect. I often mix it with hand appliqué for even more texture and dimension. RADIATING DRESDEN PLATES bargello reverse appliqué and GONE FISHING combine landscape and both hand and bargello reverse appliqué.

When writing this book, I assumed that quilters who would be drawn to it would be familiar with quilting techniques and terminology, already knowing the basics of piecing, machine appliqué, joining blocks, adding borders, quilting, and finishing.

The stress here is on the three techniques of adding bargello to your quilts. "Bargello buddies" are the fabrics that are chosen for the strip-sets that become the bargello bits. They need to play off one another without getting lost. The "straights" are the fabrics chosen to complement the bargello or chosen first as the feature fabric, guiding the choice of the bargello buddy fabrics.

Be flexible with your fabric choices. Be willing to make one bargello sequence first, make adjustments as necessary, and then make the rest of your quilt. Buy that wild fabric you've been dying to try or pull it out of your stash. Bargello may be the perfect place for it.

Each project has a different bargello sequence mapped out for it. Take the bargello sequence for the half-square triangle units and put it into a favorite block pattern of your choice. See what you come up with. Have fun on your journey through these fun and fabulous projects!

Fabric Selection

What kind of fabrics do you love? Do you love a large and wild print that you're dying to use somehow? Do you love that group of batiks that is just begging to be cut up? I've gone both ways with fabric selection—starting with the main fabric or starting with the fabrics I want in the bargello bits. I've made a fair share of quilts that I would consider "dogs," and I know it was because my fabric selection could have been much better. Not every fabric will work well in bargello but every fabric will work well in a *Bits of Bargello* quilt!

Bargello Buddies

Bargello buddies are the fabrics that hang out next to each other in a bargello bit. The easiest way to select bargello buddies is to walk into a quilt shop and grab a roll of fat quarters with all the same textured print in tons of different colorways. It's easy to select bargello buddies from your stash as well. First, identify a couple colors that you would like to play with. Then look for 5–10 fabrics that work those two colors together well. Try it. Any two colors. When selecting fabric, think of saturation of color, textures, prints with both colors in them, even different styles of fabrics—'30s style and batiks. This is an equal-opportunity fabric selection; mix it up.

You want your bargello buddies to make sense. Tie your bargello buddies together; don't just randomly choose five fabrics because they all happen to go with your straight (background) fabric in some way. It will be too choppy. If your straight fabric is a large print with a large repeat (an image recurs less frequently in the yardage), select smaller prints or textures for your bargello buddies.

Let's Talk Straights

The other fabrics to consider in these quilts are the straights. A straight is the feature fabric chosen to complement the bargello or it's the fabric that's chosen first, guiding the selection of the bargello buddies.

You'll need to find additional straight fabrics that play well with each other. You want them to take a supporting role to your main straight fabric and not distract from the bargello. Don't play it safe. Look to your main straight fabric for color combinations and amounts of color. If your primary straight fabric has a tiny little bit of brown going through it, use a tiny bit of brown in your secondary straight fabrics.

Remember when selecting your fabrics that everything has a purpose in the quilt. Love every fabric you put in it!

Buddies and Straights Team Up

Make sure that there is enough difference in texture or scale of print so the bargello will show up against the background. Bargello buddy fabrics with the same color background as the straight fabric background can be a problem. The bargello will get lost.

One way to see if things work is to take strips or fat quarters of your potential bargello buddies and lay them out on your straight. Look at the arrangement through a reducing lens or my favorite tool, the ColorScope™ Color Selector (see Resources, page 94). Viewing through this little kaleidoscope chops up the fabrics the way they'll be chopped up in your bargello so you can get a better idea of what they'll look like together.

In your pursuit of the ultimate bargello buddies, remember that textures are fabulous, but watch their scale. You are cutting these things down to about an inch. Different scales of texture can be distracting next to each other, especially if they have different contrasting colors running through them.

Not enough contrast may weaken your overall bargello. Arrange your potential bargello buddies into a gradation of color—light to dark or from one color to the next. Are they too blendy? Can you see the difference between them? If not, pull every other one out or rearrange one or two, so it's not light to dark. If the fabrics are too close together, the bargello will tend to look flat and lifeless and not too exciting.

If you have a couple of bargello buddies that are your favorites, make sure they fall in the center of any sequence because the first and last bargello buddies of the sequences won't occur as often in the bargello bit.

Building Bargello Bits

Cutting, Sewing, and Pressing Your Bargello Buddies

I love fat quarters for bargello buddies. I can easily collect them and buy a few extra in case the first choices blend too much. For cutting, they work great! I do not like to cut or sew a long strip of anything. I like working with shorter strips and I alternate the direction I sew the strips together to prevent the strip-set from distorting.

Always make a bargello buddy key by taping a piece of each buddy onto a piece of paper and numbering them according to how you plan to position them. This saves so much time in the long run.

Bargello Buddy Key

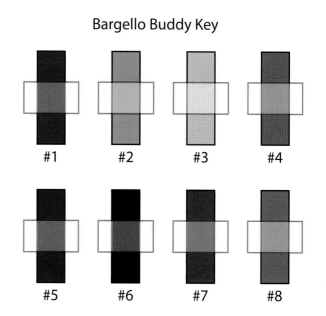

#1   #2   #3   #4

#5   #6   #7   #8

Use a smaller-than-usual stitch length when sewing any part of the bargello unit—both the strip-sets and when joining the bargello segments. Remember, you will be sewing, pressing, cutting, sewing, and pressing some more and you want it to stay together!

Press the seams open on your bargello buddy strip-sets. The open seams help stabilize the strip-set. You don't get that little ridge at the seam as when the seam allowance is pressed to one side, and your quilt will lie flatter.

I use a scant ¼" seam allowance when sewing the bargello segments together. Usually, I'll sew every other seam of the bargello sequence, stop to press the seams open, then sew the remaining seams. If I am using a scant ¼", I don't catch the seam allowance when sewing the next seam, even on the narrowest ¾" segments, but still have enough allowance to press open.

Use a pressing cloth when you are pressing bargello. There are lots of high and low areas because of all the seams, so bargello needs a lot of pressing. Any of the highs will start to get shiny from the heat of the iron. I also highly recommend starch and steam. I do my best to make sure I cut accurately and sew accurately. But with all the piecing going on here, things can easily get out of shape.

Remember that term "blocking?" It allows you to manipulate your quilt or pieces of your quilt to fit a certain size. Your blocks can be convinced they are whatever size you think they should be—just use steam and starch!

Stepping the Bargello

I am looking to create unexpected movement and color interest when I place bargello in a quilt. This is done by off-setting the bargello segments to create the pattern and movement.

When arranging the segments in a sequence, designate a bargello buddy to establish the segment's position. When a figure shows that a segment is ½ step down from the adjacent segment, that means to line up the top of the designated bargello buddy in the second segment to about the middle of the same bargello buddy in the first segment.

"About" is the operative word here. Throw away your seam ripper! Do your best to line up the segments as I have indicated. The offset steps of the bargello are given with each project so that the sequence fits into the designated area on the quilt. There is always a little room to "fudge" a bit so if a segment looks more like ¾ of a step than ½ step, you really don't need to remove the stitching. There's enough wiggle room built in.

Looping the Bargello

Another way of creating movement is to loop the bargello segments, which is done by sewing the first bargello buddy to the last, right sides together. The pattern will indicate where to unseam the loops. This gives an even edge to the bargello sequence.

Looping is done in the PINWHEELS & PYRAMIDS and RADIATING DRESDEN PLATES projects. Looping individual segments is just as fast and more accurate than looping an entire strip-set first and then cutting the segments.

Favorite Things

This is a list of sewing tools that I find extremely helpful to use (see Resources, page 94):

ColorScope™ Color Selector—This little gadget from Cottage Mills is so useful when choosing bargello buddies. Spread out your straight fabric, lay your potential bargello buddies on top, and look through the ColorScope to see how they work together.

Large roll of tracing paper

Spray starch—Buy the squirt-bottle kind, not the aerosol. You really need this to get your bargello to lie flat!

Freezer paper—I buy this on 150' rolls and use it for templates.

Appliqué scissors—The kind with a wide lip on one blade prevents cutting the wrong fabric when trimming.

Stabilizer—I always use this for machine appliqué, especially beneath the bargello. My favorite kind is Ricky Tims' Stable Stuff® Poly in 8½" x 11" sheets.

Hot steam iron—Nothing like a good iron with a lot of steam! I can convince anything, between the steam and the spray starch, to stay where I want it!

X-ray film/plastic—I use X-ray film for both appliqué placement and doodling for machine quilting. I use a dry-erase marker and trace the appliqué design, then lay it over my background fabric while I'm positioning the individual pieces. For machine quilting, I lay the X-ray film over the block or quilt I'm thinking about and doodle designs with a dry-erase marker. This way I can see what the design looks like before I quilt it.

Plastic sheet protectors—These hold my bargello pieces when I'm jumping from project to project, and are an inexpensive plastic overlay for smaller projects.

Appliqué Techniques

For any appliqué, I use an "overlay"—a tracing of the design on X-ray film or clear plastic—to note where the appliqué pieces overlap and where the pieces lie in relation to the other pieces and the block as a whole. This ensures accurate placement.

I will use both hand and machine appliqué in the same piece. This gives added dimension to the appliqué. The hand appliqué has a tendency to poof up a bit, while the machine appliqué lies flat.

Hand Appliqué
Trace the appliqué shapes onto freezer paper. These templates can be reused. Cut out the appliqué shapes on the drawn lines. With a dry iron, press the freezer-paper templates to the RIGHT side of your chosen appliqué fabrics. Cut out the fabric appliqué shapes, 1/8"–1/4" beyond the edge of the freezer paper.

On a flat surface, position the plastic overlay on the background fabric. Slide the appliqué pieces into place, matching the traced lines. Remove the overlay and secure the pieces with pins or basting.

Using the edge of the freezer paper as a guide, appliqué the pieces into place using the needle-turn method.

Bargello as Reverse Appliqué
I like to replace certain parts of an appliqué design with bits of bargello. For example, only parts of the appliquéd fish in GONE FISHING are replaced with reverse-appliqué bargello.

For reverse appliqué, start by tracing the shapes onto freezer paper and cutting them out. Position the freezer paper on the background fabric and press in place with a dry iron. Staystitch around the shape right at the edge of the freezer paper. This will keep the background fabric from stretching out of shape. Peel off the freezer paper and save to reuse. Cut the background fabric away just inside the staystitching, making sure to cut in a smooth line as you will be using this as a guideline for your machine-appliqué stitching.

Position the bargello sequence under the background opening, right-sides up, and pin or baste in place.

Place stabilizer beneath and appliqué over the staystitching with a narrow machine satin stitch.

If you choose to do the reverse appliqué by needle-turning the raw edges of the background piece by hand, make sure to take very small stitches and go all the way through the bargello with your needle. Just grabbing the top fabric won't hold it in place.

Trim away the excess bargello from the back, leaving a ¼"–⅜" seam allowance. I like to use the appliqué scissors with the lip on one blade for this task. It helps prevent accidentally cutting through the background.

Adding Borders

Cut the number of strips needed according to your pattern instructions. Cut across the width of the border fabric unless otherwise indicated.

Measure the width of your quilt through the center.

Sew enough strips together to cut two pieces equal to the width measurement.

Fold the border strips in half and mark with a pin.

Fold the quilt in half and mark the top and bottom center points with a pin.

Pin the border strips to the top and bottom, right sides together, starting in the center and easing in any extra fabric. Sew and press the seams toward the border.

Measure the length of the quilt through the center including the top and bottom borders.

Sew the remaining strips together and cut two pieces equal to the length measurement.

In the same manner, mark the centers of the strips and the quilt sides, and add the side borders. Press the seams toward the border.

Let's Play Ball!

31" x 38½", made by the author

There's lots of baseball nostalgia here in upstate New York. The birthplace of Abner Doubleday (regarded as the father of baseball) is only five miles from me, and Cooperstown, site of the Baseball Hall of Fame, is less than two hours away.

This is a different kind of landscape quilt. Any of you who have young kids spend tons of time at ball fields. As most of you can attest, the most movement at a ball field is in the stands. There's lots of time for hand appliqué, but make sure you are not looking down when your #1 player makes a huge play!

This quilt has bargello inserted as the fans. When choosing your bargello buddies, go for your favorite team colors—O.K. your kid's favorite team colors. Once you've identified those, choose some shades of those colors. Tread carefully here! Don't start shading towards another team.

With this bargello, mix up the buddies and go for contrasts. Other fabrics you need to think about are a sky fabric, fabrics for the stadium lights, and the ball field. Use a dark fabric without much print for the silhouette.

Fabrics & Supplies

½ yard dark sky
½ yard yellow (for stadium lights)
⅛ yard each 8 bargello buddies
⅓ yard background
¼ yard grass fabric
¼ yard infield
¼ inner border
⅝ yard outer border (1½ yards if fabric is directional)
12" x 12" square of dark fabric (for baseball silhouette)
1¼ yards backing
35" x 43" batting
¼ yard binding
freezer paper
stabilizer

Stadium Lights

Draw 2 rectangles 10½" x 11½" on freezer paper. Add the diagonal lines and section labels (see templates, page 17).

Cut freezer paper apart on the lines (fig. 1). Lay the light segments on the back of the stadium lights fabric and the others on the back of the dark sky fabric. Cut out with a ¼" seam allowance on all sides.

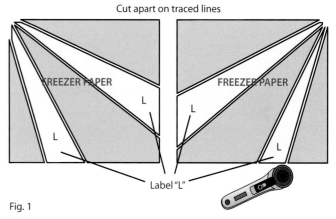

Cut apart on traced lines

Label "L"

Fig. 1

Keep the freezer paper in place as a guideline and for stability. Place right sides together and sew the segments together. Press the seams open. Peel off the freezer paper. Sew the two blocks together and press the seam open. Set aside.

Piecing the Bargello

Determine the layout of your 8 bargello buddies and make a key, numbering the bargello buddies from the top down.

Cut 1 strip of each bargello buddy fabric as follows:

Bargello Buddy	Cut Strip Width
1 & 2	3"
3 & 4	2½"
5 & 6	2"
7 & 8	1½"

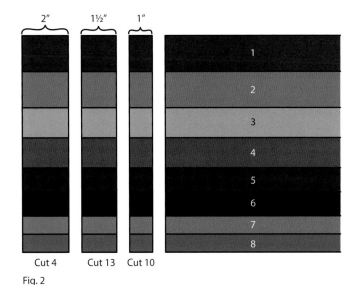

Cut 4   Cut 13   Cut 10

Fig. 2

Cut each strip in half, so the lengths are at least 20". Sew into 2 strip-sets, alternating the direction you sew the seams. Press the seams open.

For the bargello sequence, cut the segments as follows (fig. 2).
4 segments 2"
13 segments 1½"
10 segments 1"

Arrange the segments in the sequence shown in figure 3 (page 13), always keeping bargello buddy #1 at the top. When identifying a "step" up or down, use the designated bargello buddy.

Sew the segments together. Press the seams open.

Quilt Top Assembly

Draw the bargello, outfield, and infield templates on a large piece of freezer paper at least 23" x 23", starting with two rectangles 11" x 22" and 6" x 22" drawn 3" apart as shown (fig. 4).

Tape two or more pieces of freezer paper together to get the overall size you need. Use a compass or a pencil and piece of string to draw the arcs (ABC, DEF, and GHI).

Label the bargello, outfield, and infield templates and cut out on the drawn lines.

With a dry iron, center the bargello template onto the bargello sequence and cut out with a rotary cutter or scissors, leaving a ¼" seam allowance on all sides.

Cut 2 rectangles 4" x 8" of background fabric. Sew to the sides of the bargello (fig. 5). Press the seams toward the background.

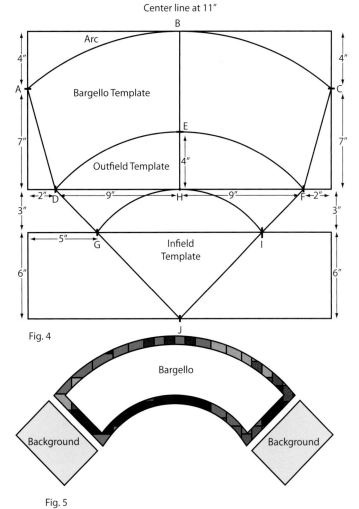

Fig. 4

Fig. 5

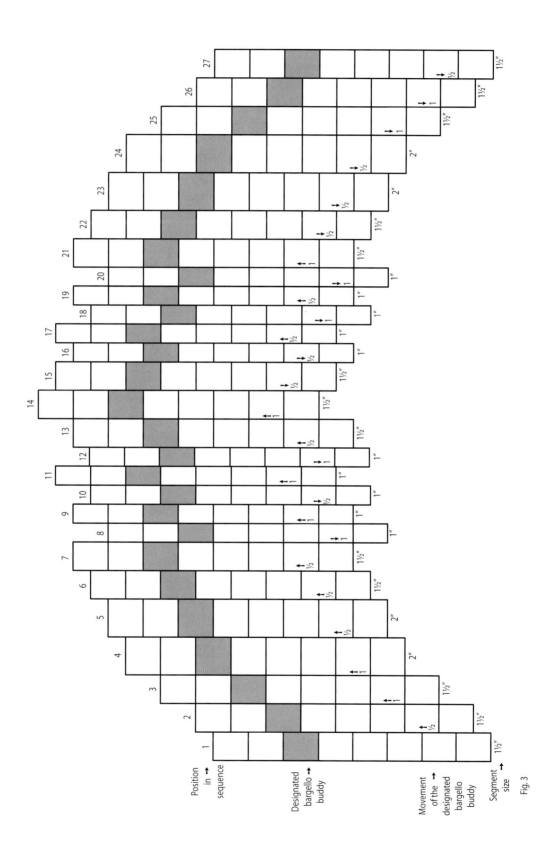

Fig. 3

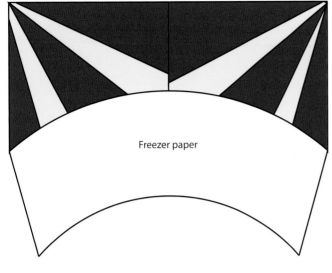

Fig. 6

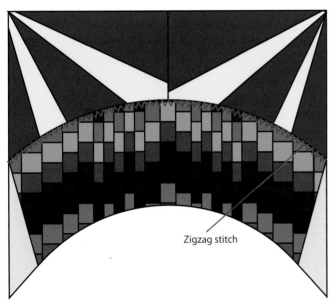

Zigzag stitch

Fig. 7

Peel off the freezer-paper bargello template and center it over the stadium lights blocks, with the top corners touching both sides (fig. 6). Press in place and staystitch along the edge of the template. Remove the freezer paper and trim the lights ⅛" from the staystitching.

Lay the bargello sequence along the staystitching, position stabilizer beneath, and machine appliqué in place (fig. 7). Trim the background even with the edges of the stadium lights.

In the same manner add the outfield and infield, matching the thread to the fabric of the newest addition.

Trim the background even with the outfield as shown in the quilt top assembly on page 15.

Cut a 13" x 13" square of background fabric in half on the diagonal. Sew the triangles to the lower two corners, as shown on page 15. Press the seams. Appliqué the baseball diamond and bases in position.

Square up the top to 22½" x 26½".

Add a 7½" border to the bottom and a 5½" border to the top of the quilt. Press.

Enlarge and trace the silhouette (page 16) onto freezer paper. Cut out on the drawn line. Press on the right side of the dark fabric. Cut out leaving a ⅛"–¼" seam allowance. Appliqué to the quilt using a needle-turn method and the freezer-paper template as a guide.

Add a 2½" inner border to the sides and a 3½" outer border to the sides.

Quilt and bind as desired.

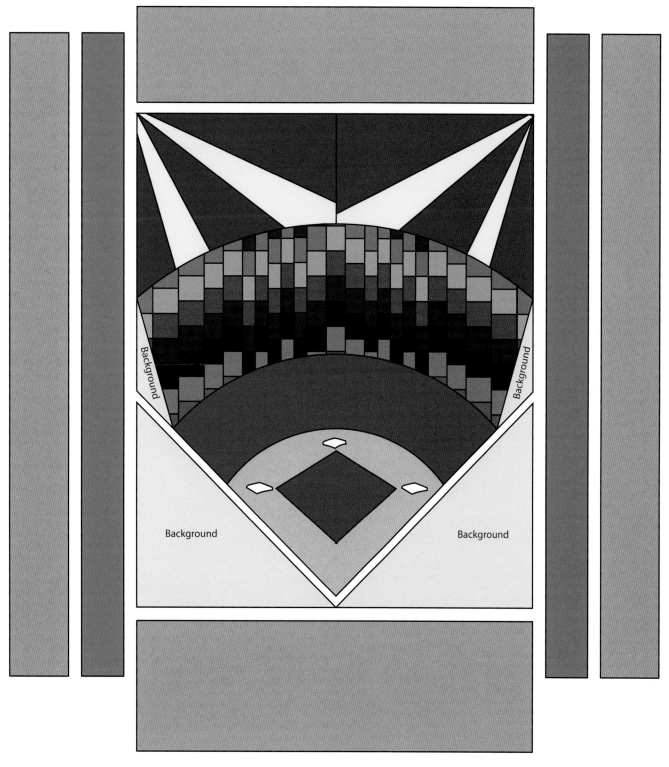

Quilt top assembly

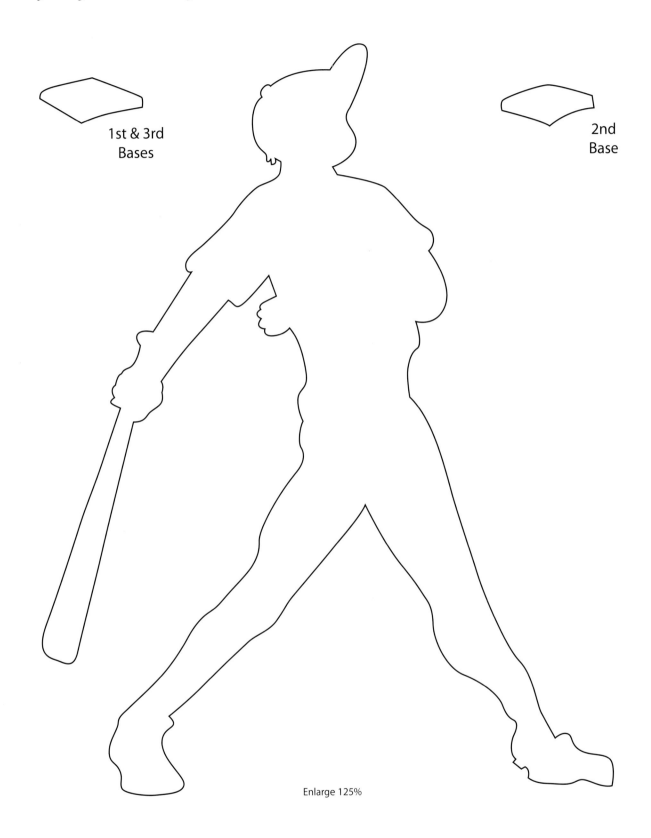

1st & 3rd
Bases

2nd
Base

Enlarge 125%

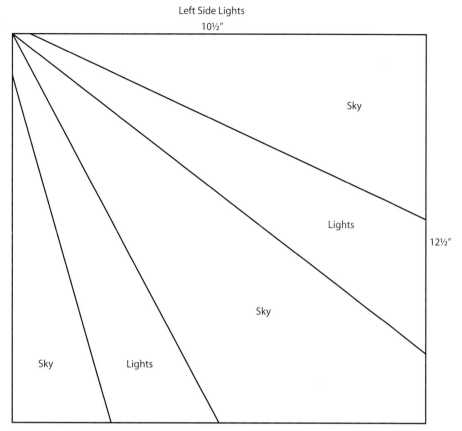

Left Side Lights

10½″

Sky

Lights

12½″

Sky

Sky   Lights

Enlarge 255%

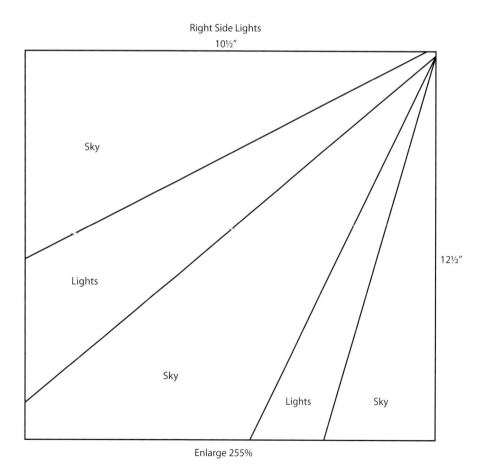

Right Side Lights

10½″

Sky

Lights

12½″

Sky

Lights   Sky

Enlarge 255%

Adirondack Windows

32" x 37", made by the author

We live in upstate New York at the base of the Adirondack Mountains, which are more green and rolling than rocky and mountainous. Glens Falls, a city north of me and home to my favorite quilt guild, Wings Falls Quilters, has a yearly balloon fest. The number of gorgeous hot air balloons you can see at one time is amazing.

This quilt puts the bargello in the landscape as green rolling hills. There are four bargello sequences in this quilt. When selecting your bargello buddies, choose lots of shades and textures of greens (love those fat quarters!). Just make sure the bargello buddy fabrics don't blend too much with their neighbors. Keep in mind that bargello sequence 1 (the closest hill) should be darker in appearance than bargello sequence 4 (the farthest hill).

Cut your bargello buddies across the widest portion of the fat quarters, perpendicular to the selvage.

Fabrics & Supplies

8–12 fat quarter bargello buddies for bargello sequences 1, 2, and 4
⅛ yard each 9 bargello buddies for bargello sequence 3
1 fat quarter sky fabric
⅛ yard light molding
⅛ yard dark molding
¼ yard window sashing fabric—mid-tone, between the light and dark molding
⅛ yard for window sill
⅛ yard edge of window sill—lighter than sill
1 yard border and binding fabric that imitates wallpaper—can be a directional stripe
scraps for balloon appliqué
1¼ yards backing
36" x 41" batting
embroidery floss for balloon ropes
stabilizer & freezer paper
matching threads for machine and hand appliqué

Piecing the Bargello
Bargello Sequence 1
Determine the layout of 10 bargello buddies for the closest hill and make a key. This should be the darkest sequence.

Cut 1 strip 1¾" x 20" of each of the bargello buddies (total 10). Sew into a strip-set, alternating the direction you sew the seams. Press the seams open.

For bargello sequence 1, cut the segments as follows (fig. 1, page 20):
2 segments 2½"
8 segments 1½"

Arrange the segments as shown (fig. 2, page 20).

Sew the segments together. Press the seams open. Set aside.

Bargello Sequence 2
Determine the layout of 8 bargello buddies for the next (second) hill and make a key.

Cut 1 strip 1¾" x 20" of each of the bargello buddies (total 8). Sew into a strip-set, alternating the direction you sew the seams. Press the seams open.

For bargello sequence 2, cut the segments as follows (fig. 3, page 21):
2 segments 3½"
3 segments 2½"
3 segments 1½"

Arrange the segments as shown (fig. 4, page 21).

Sew the segments together. Press the seams open. Set aside.

Landscape Projects — Adirondack Windows

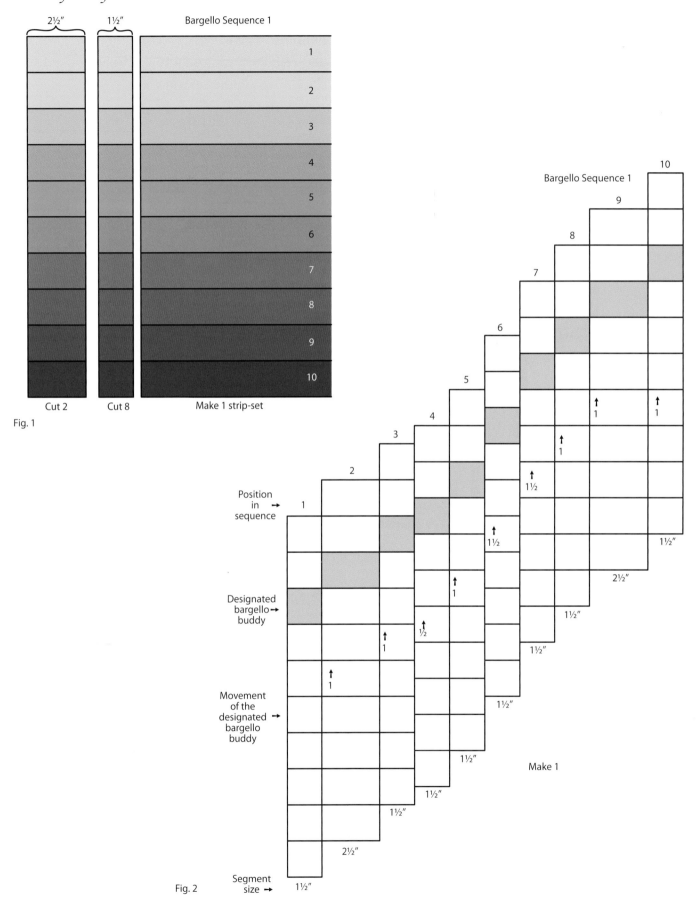

2½" 1½" Bargello Sequence 1

1
2
3
4
5
6
7
8
9
10

Cut 2   Cut 8   Make 1 strip-set

Fig. 1

Bargello Sequence 1

10
9
8
7
6
5
4
3
2
1

Position in sequence →

Designated bargello buddy →

Movement of the designated bargello buddy →

↑1   ↑1   1½"
↑1   2½"
↑1½   1½"
↑1½   1½"
↑1   1½"
↑½   1½"
↑1   1½"
↑1   1½"
1½"
2½"

Make 1

Segment size →   1½"

Fig. 2

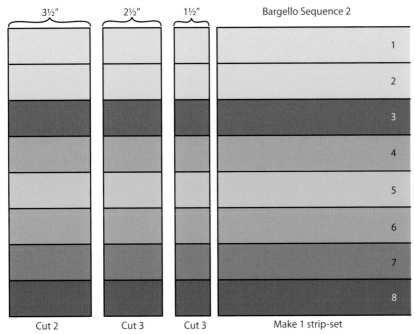

Bargello Sequence 2

3½"   2½"   1½"

1
2
3
4
5
6
7
8

Cut 2   Cut 3   Cut 3   Make 1 strip-set

Fig. 3

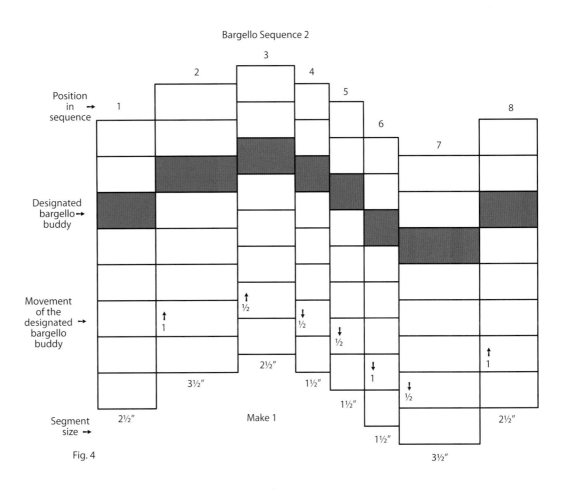

Bargello Sequence 2

Position in sequence →   1   2   3   4   5   6   7   8

Designated bargello buddy →

Movement of the designated bargello buddy →   ↑1   ↑½   ↓½   ↓½   ↓1   ↑1   ↓½

Segment size →   2½"   3½"   2½"   1½"   1½"   1½"   3½"   2½"

Make 1

Fig. 4

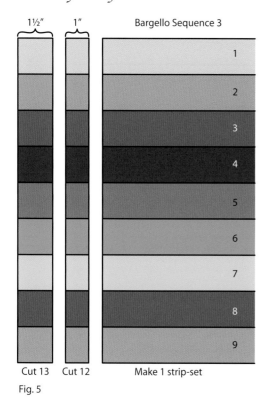

1½"   1"   Bargello Sequence 3

Cut 13   Cut 12   Make 1 strip-set

Fig. 5

Bargello Sequence 3

Determine the layout of 9 bargello buddies for the next (third) hill and make a key.

Cut 1 strip 1½" wide of each of the bargello buddies (total 9). Sew into a strip-set, alternating the direction you sew the seams. Press the seams open.

For bargello sequence 3, cut the segments as follows (fig. 5):
13 segments 1½"
12 segments 1"

Arrange the segments as shown (fig. 6, page 23).

Sew the segments together. Press the seams open. Set aside.

Bargello Sequence 4

Determine the layout of 7 bargello buddies for the farthest hill and make a key. This should be the lightest sequence.

Cut 1 strip 1¾" x 20" of each of the bargello buddies (total 7). Sew into a strip-set, alternating the direction you sew the seams. Press the seams open.

For bargello sequence 4, cut the segments as follows (fig. 7):
1 segment 2½"
2 segments 2"
4 segments 1½"
2 segments 1"

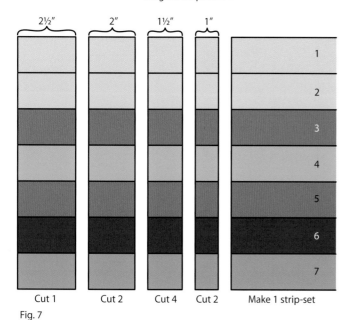

Bargello Sequence 4

2½"   2"   1½"   1"

Cut 1   Cut 2   Cut 4   Cut 2   Make 1 strip-set

Fig. 7

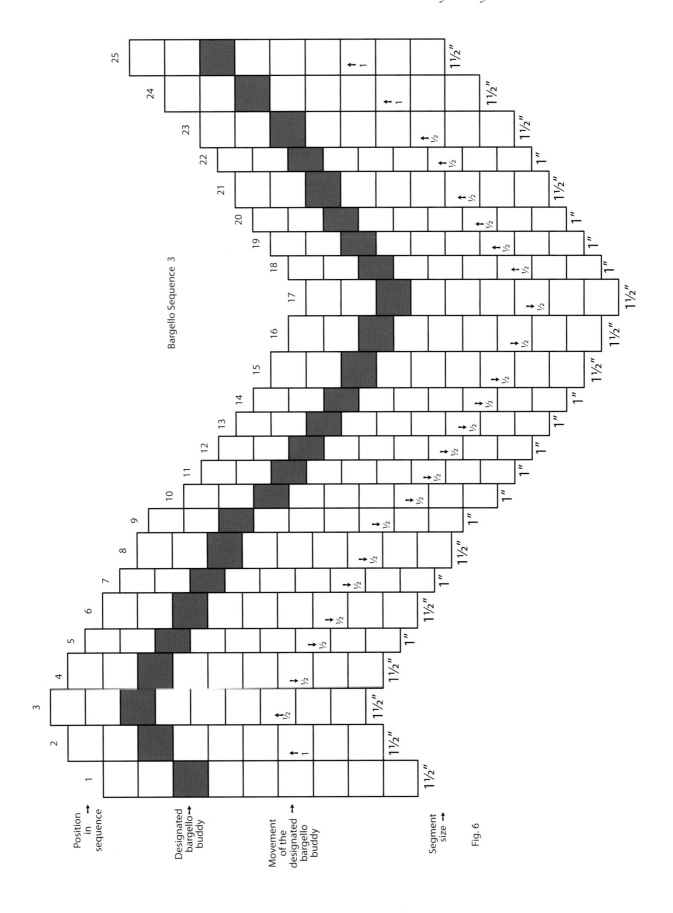

Bargello Sequence 3

Fig. 6

Position in sequence

Designated bargello buddy

Movement of the designated bargello buddy

Segment size

Arrange the segments as shown (fig. 8).

Sew the segments together. Press the seams open. Set aside.

Quilt Assembly

Cut a rectangle 14½" x 19½" of sky fabric.

With your rotary cutter, trim off the jagged top edge of each of the hill sequences, following the hill shape of each (fig. 9).

Position the farthest hill (bargello sequence 4) over the sky fabric. Pin in place. Place stabilizer beneath and machine appliqué in place matching the thread to the bargello buddies (fig. 10, page

25). Remove the excess stabilizer. Position the next hill (sequence 3) and pin in place. Machine appliqué as before. Trim the excess sequence 4 bargello from underneath. Position the remaining hill sequences (the second, then the closest) and repeat these steps to sew them in place as shown in figure 10.

Square up the hills and sky assembly to 18½" x 19½".

Trace balloon pieces (page 29) onto freezer paper. Cut out on the traced lines. Press freezer-paper templates to the right sides of chosen fabrics. Refer to the quilt photo (page 18) for positioning. Using a needle-turn method

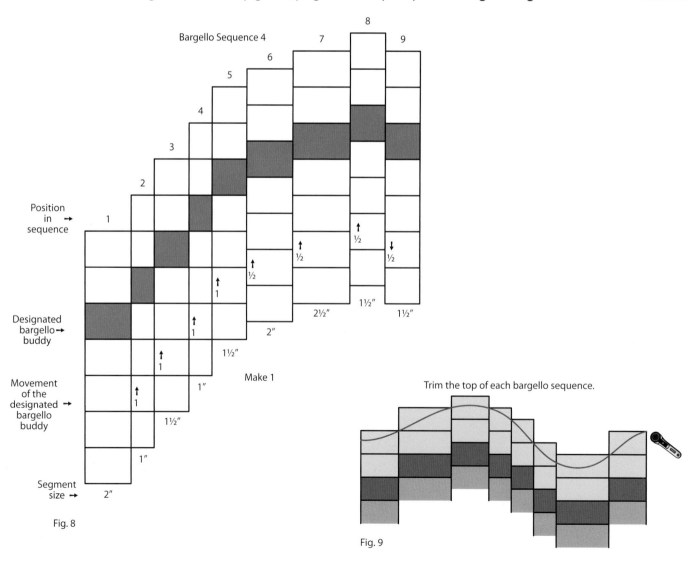

Fig. 8

Make 1

Fig. 9

Trim the top of each bargello sequence.

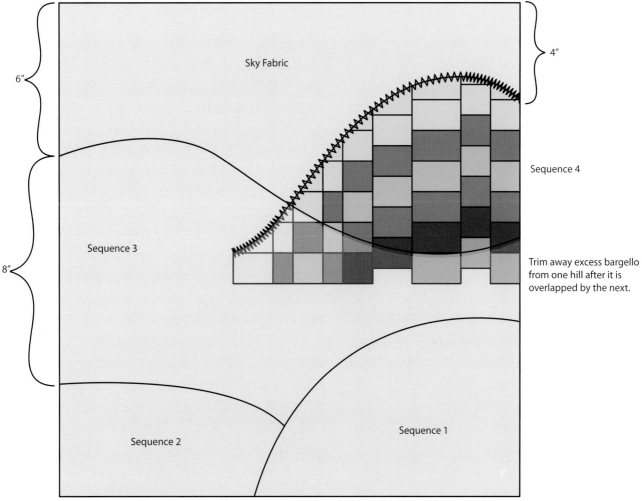

Fig. 10. Hill placement: measurements are approximate.

Labels within figure:
- 6″
- 8″
- 4″
- Sky Fabric
- Sequence 4
- Sequence 3
- Sequence 2
- Sequence 1
- Trim away excess bargello from one hill after it is overlapped by the next.

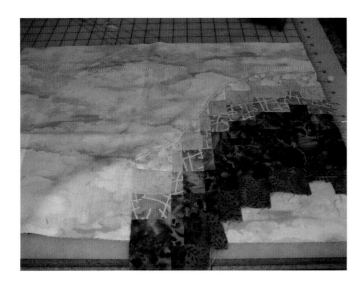

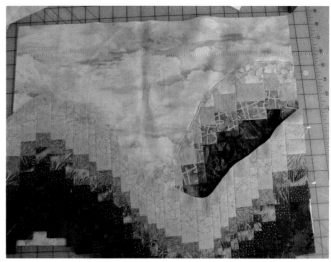

of appliqué and the freezer paper as a guide, stitch into place. (See Appliqué Techniques, page 8.) Peel off the freezer paper. Using a chain stitch, embroider ropes on the balloons. Use a satin stitch to embroider the baskets. You may want to hand appliqué the largest basket.

Sashing and Borders

Cut a square 4¼" x 4¼" of both the sashing and light molding fabrics. Make 2 half-square triangles.

Square up the half-square triangles to measure 3½" x 3½". Trim one to a 2½" x 3½" rectangle as shown (fig. 11).

Cut a strip 2½" x 18½" of the sashing fabric. Fold in both long edges ¼" and press. Position across the middle of the window 11½" from the top edge and pin. Hand appliqué in place.

Cut 1 strip 1½" x 19½" of dark molding fabric and sew to the left side of the quilt.

Cut 2 strips of sashing fabric:
2½" x 19½"
3½" x 19½"

Sew the narrow strip to the top of the quilt and the wide strip to the bottom.

Cut a 3½" x 19½" strip of light molding and add the rectangle and half-square triangle to the top and bottom as shown on page 27. Add the molding to the right side of the quilt.

Cut a 2½" x 22½" strip of window sill fabric. Cut a 1½" x 22½" strip of window sill edge fabric. Sew the strips together and press. Sew to the bottom edge of the quilt. Press.

Cut the border fabric into 4 strips 5½" wide. Pay attention to the pattern when you cut the strips to maintain the look of wallpaper. Add to the quilt.

Designer's note: This potted plant helps to give perspective and show the viewer that they are looking through a window. If you're not fond of this particular plant, try some geraniums for a splash of color.

Trace the ivy leaves, flower pot, and dirt onto freezer paper (pages 28–29). Cut out on traced lines. Press the freezer-paper templates to the right sides of your chosen fabrics. Position as shown (see quilt photo, page 18) and using a needle-turn method of appliqué and the freezer paper as a guide, stitch into place. Peel off the freezer paper.

Quilting

ADIRONDACK WINDOWS is a lot of fun to quilt because there is so much going on. Stitch some air movement in the sky. Add some grass to the hills. Inside echo the sill and moldings—stitch in the ditch to pop those out a bit. Do some vertical quilting on the wallpaper.

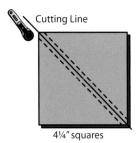

Cutting Line

4¼" squares

Fig. 11

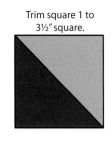

Trim square 1 to 3½" square.

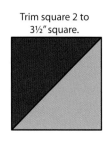

Trim square 2 to 3½" square.

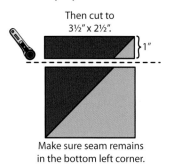

Then cut to 3½" x 2½".

1"

Make sure seam remains in the bottom left corner.

Quilt top assembly

Leaves

Freezer Paper template

right side of fabric

⅛"-¼" seam allowance

overlay "dirt" making sure to leave the rim showing

Applique terracotta pot on first

Applique leaves – make sure to spill some over the shelf.

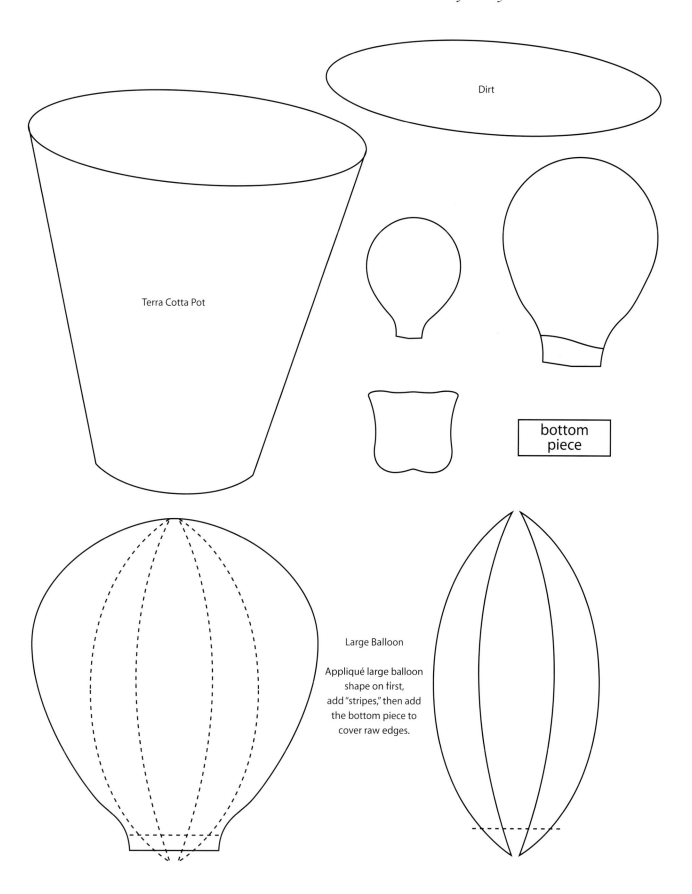

Dirt

Terra Cotta Pot

bottom
piece

Large Balloon

Appliqué large balloon
shape on first,
add "stripes," then add
the bottom piece to
cover raw edges.

Moonstone Flower

72" x 90", made by the author

This quilt is made of simple recognizable blocks set in a traditional manner, stirred up with bits of bargello. The MOONSTONE FLOWER block is based on a Nine-Patch assembly with each of the nine "patches" measuring 6" finished. These bargello units can easily be used in any Nine-Patch design.

BITS *of* Bargello – Karen Gibbs

Make sure to place your favorite bargello buddy fabrics at the center of the bargello strip-sets. Bargello buddies #1 and #6 do not show as much.

Fabrics & Supplies

⅝ yard each of 6 bargello buddy fabrics
2⅛ yards light background fabric
2 yards of straight fabric #1 (for
     the main block and border)
1⅜ yards straight fabric #2 (for
     the 9½" x 9½" squares)
1 yard of straight fabric #3 (for
     four-patch units and border)
1 yard of straight fabric #4 (for
     four-patch units and border)
5¼ yards backing
⅔ yard binding
80" x 98" batting

There are three bargello sequences in this quilt—sequence 1 for the pinwheels, sequence 2 for the flower petals, and sequence 3 for the 3½" x 3½" flower buds.

Moonstone Flower Blocks

Determine the layout of your bargello buddies and make a key.

Designer's Note: Instead of arranging the bargello buddies from light to dark, mixing the light and darks works best for this quilt.

Cut each bargello buddy into 13 strips 1½" wide. Cut each strip in half, so the lengths are at least 20". You'll make 26 identical strip-sets, alternating the direction you sew the seams. Press the seams open. (The number of strip-sets needed for each sequence is indicated in figures 1, 5, and 8.)

Designer's Note: I find half-length strips easier to handle. If you don't cut your strips in half, you only need 13 strip-sets.

Pinwheels

For each bargello sequence 1, cut the segments as follows (fig. 1):
1 segment 1¾" (12 total)
2 segments 1½" (24 total)
2 segments 1¼" (24 total)

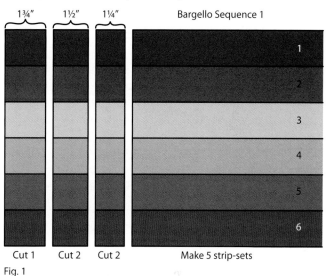

Fig. 1

Arrange the segments for each sequence as shown (fig. 2).

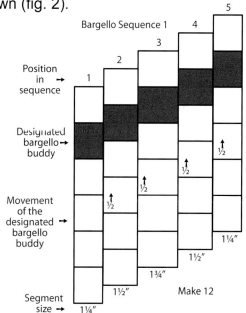

Fig. 2

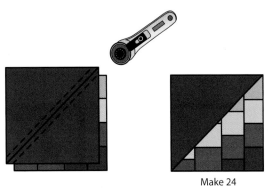

Fig. 3

Make 24

Sew the segments together; press the seams open. Make 12 bargello sequences.

Trim each bargello sequence to measure 4¼" x 4¼" .

Cut 12 squares 4¼" x 4¼" of straight fabric #1.

Make 24 half-square triangles with the bargello and straight fabric squares (fig. 3). Square up to measure 3½" x 3½".

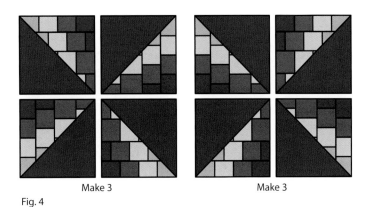

Make 3   Make 3

Fig. 4

Arrange 4 half-square triangles in each pinwheel and join as shown (fig. 4) to make 6 pinwheels. Press the seams open.

Flower Petals

For each bargello sequence 2, cut the segments as follows (fig. 5):
1 segment 1½" (24 total)
4 segments 1¼" (96 total)

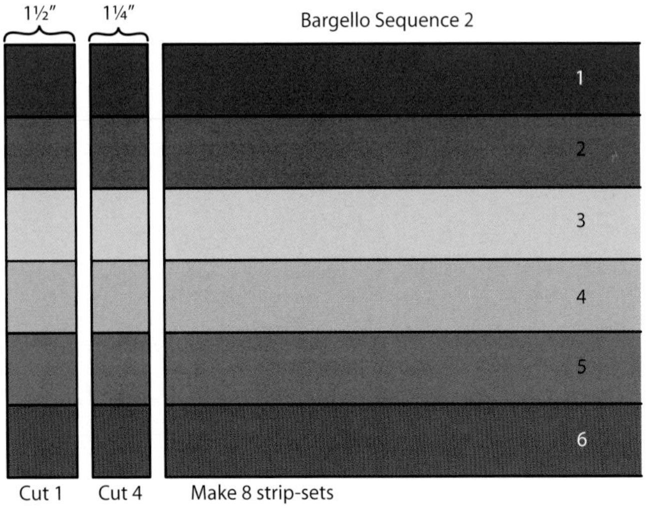

Arrange the segments for each sequence as shown (fig. 6):

1½"   1¼"   Bargello Sequence 2

1
2
3
4
5
6

Cut 1   Cut 4   Make 8 strip-sets

Fig. 5

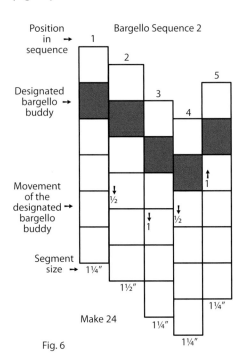

Position in sequence →

Bargello Sequence 2

Designated bargello buddy →

Movement of the designated bargello buddy →

Segment size →   1¼"

1½"

1¼"

Make 24   1¼"   1¼"

Fig. 6

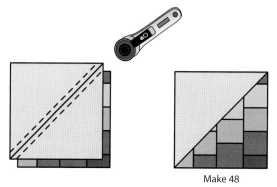

Sew the segments together; press the seams open. Make 24 bargello sequences.

Trim each bargello sequence to measure 4¼"x 4¼".

Cut 24 squares 4¼" x 4¼" of background fabric.

Make 48 half-square triangles with the bargello and background fabric squares (fig. 7). Press toward the straight fabric. Square up to measure 3½" x 3½". Set aside.

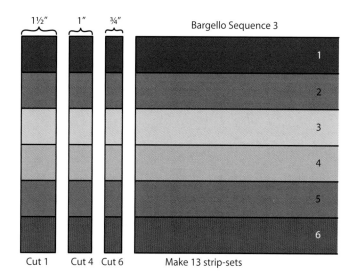

Make 48

Fig. 7

Flower Buds

For each bargello sequence 3, cut the segments as follows (fig. 8):
1 segment 1½" (24 total)
4 segments 1" (96 total)
6 segments ¾" (144 total)

1½" 1" ¾"   Bargello Sequence 3

1
2
3
4
5
6

Cut 1 Cut 4 Cut 6   Make 13 strip-sets

Fig. 8

Bargello Sequence 3

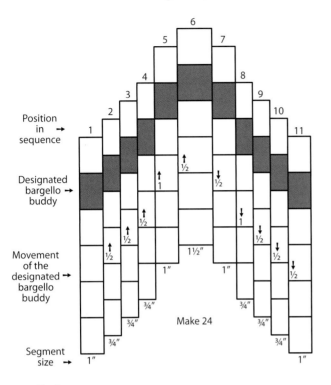

Fig. 9

Arrange the segments for each sequence as shown (fig. 9).

Sew the segments together; press the seams open. Make 24 bargello sequences.

Using a square ruler, cut each sequence into an on-point 3½" x 3½" square as shown (fig. 10). Line up the top of the ruler with the top of the second bargello buddy, centered on the 1½" segment. Check all sides of the square before you cut. Set the bargello squares aside.

Moonstone Flower Block Corner Assembly

Cut 24 squares 3½" x 3½" of background fabric.

Arrange the bargello sequence 2 half-square triangles, on-point squares, and background squares and join as shown (fig. 11) to make 24 Flower blocks. Press the seams away from the bargello or press them open.

Bargello Sequence 3

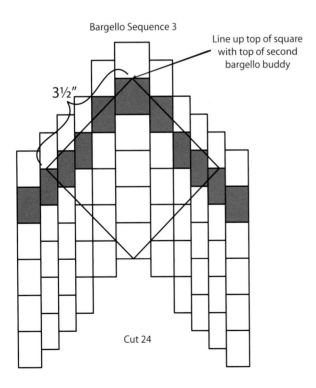

Fig. 10

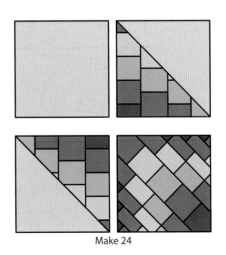

Make 24

Fig. 11

Moonstone Flower Block Side Units

Cut 24 squares 4¼" x 4¼" of both straight fabric #1 and background fabric (total 48).

Make 48 half-square triangles (fig. 12). Trim to measure 3½" x 3 ½".

Cut 24 rectangles 3½" x 6½" of straight fabric #1.

Arrange the half-square triangles and rectangles and join as shown (fig. 13).

Moonstone Flower Block Assembly

Arrange the units as shown (fig. 14). Join the units in rows and join the rows to complete six Moonstone Flower blocks. Press the seams away from the bargello or press them open. The blocks should measure 18½" x 18½".

Alternate Block Assembly

The alternate block is made of 2 four-patch units and 2 plain squares.

Cut 3 strips 9½" wide of straight fabric #2. Cut into 12 squares 9½" x 9½".

Cut 2 strips 5" wide of both straight fabric #3 and #4 (4 strips total).

Cut 4 strips 5" wide of background fabric.

Fig. 12

Make 48

Make 24

Fig. 13

Make 6

Fig. 14

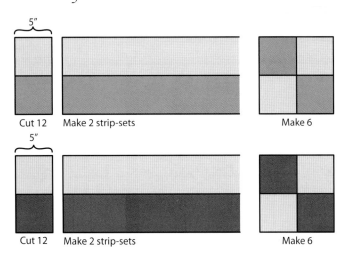

5"

Cut 12   Make 2 strip-sets   Make 6

5"

Cut 12   Make 2 strip-sets   Make 6

Fig. 15

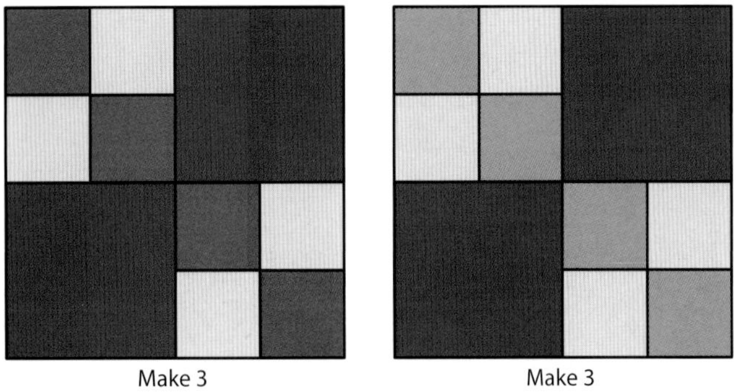

Make 4 strip-sets as shown (fig. 15). Cut into 5" segments. Assemble into 12 four-patch units. Four-patch units should measure 9½" x 9½".

Join four-patch units and 9½" squares as shown (fig. 16) to make 6 blocks. Pay attention to the position of the straight fabric and the four-patch units.

Quilt Top Assembly

Arrange the blocks as shown in the quilt top assembly (page 37). Sew the blocks into rows and join the rows.

Cornerstones and Borders

Cut 4 squares 5" x 5" and 4 squares 5½" x 5½" of background fabric.

Cut 4 squares 5" x 5" and 4 squares 5½" x 5½" of straight fabric #2.

Make 8 half-square triangle units with the 5 ½" squares. Trim to measure 5" x 5".

Make 3   Make 3

Fig. 16

Join the squares and half-square triangle units as shown for the border cornerstones (fig. 17).

Cut 7 strips 5" wide of straight fabric #1. Join into 2 strips 5" x 54½" and 2 strips 5" x 72½".

Cut 7 strips 2¾" wide of straight fabric #3. Join into 2 strips 2¾" x 54½" and 2 strips 2¾" x 72½".

Cut 7 strips 2¾" wide of straight fabric #4. Join into 2 strips 2¾" x 54½" and 2 strips 2¾" x 72½".

Sew border strips together as shown.

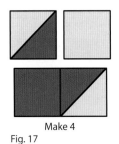

Make 4

Fig. 17

Add the 54½" top and bottom borders to the quilt top. Press the seams toward the borders. Add the border cornerstones to the ends of the side borders and add to the sides of the quilt.

Quilt As Desired

Designer's Note: Prior to quilting, I like to press the bargello with starch. This ensures that the bargello is flat and makes it easier to quilt.

Quilt top assembly

Bargello Lonestar

76" x 76", made by the author

This quilt achieves a dramatic effect with simple piecing. The bargello is pieced in long strips, joined with plain straight fabrics, and cut into rows that are sewn together to form diamonds. Four sets of bargello buddies are needed. The main colors from the bargello buddies are carried to the appliqué in the center of the leaves.

Fabrics & Supplies

⅛ yard each 6 brown bargello buddies

⅓ yard each 6 turquoise bargello buddies

⅓ yard each 6 pink bargello buddies

⅛ yard each 6 green bargello buddies

½ yard brown straight fabric

½ yard green straight fabric

1 yard turquoise straight fabric

2 yards background fabric

1¼ yards border fabric

¾ yard for the appliqué swirls

¼ yard each 2 leaf appliqué fabrics

5 yards backing

¾ yards binding

84" x 84" batting

lightweight fusible web

freezer paper

matching thread for appliqué

Bargello Assembly
Bargello Sequences 1 & 2

Except for the fabric and the number needed, these two sequences are the same.

Lay out your brown and turquoise bargello buddies from light to dark and make a key.

Cut 2 strips 1½" wide of each of the 6 brown bargello buddies. Cut the strips in half, so the lengths are at least 20".

Cut 6 strips 1½" wide of each of the 6 turquoise bargello buddies. Cut the strips in half, so the lengths are at least 20".

Sew into 4 brown and 12 turquoise strip-sets. Press the seams open. Cut into segments (fig. 1).

For each bargello sequence 1, cut 5 segments 1½" wide (total 50 plus 2 extra).

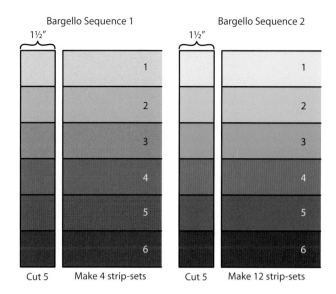

Fig. 1

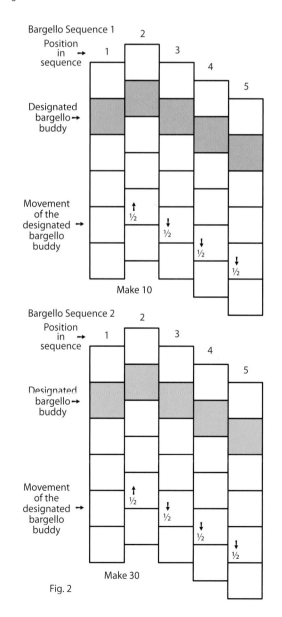

Fig. 2

For each bargello sequence 2, cut 6 segments 1½" wide (total 150 plus 6 extra).

Arrange the segments for each sequence as shown on page 39 (fig. 2).

Sew the segments together. Press the seams open.

Make 2 brown and 6 turquoise bargello strips by sewing 5 sequences plus 1 segment together, positioning the first segment of the next sequence one step up from the fifth segment of the preceding sequence (fig. 3, page 41). Press the seams open.

Bargello Sequences 3 & 4
Except for the fabric and the number needed, these two sequences are the same.

Lay out your green and pink bargello buddies from light to dark and make a key.

Cut 2 strips 1½" wide of each of the 6 green bargello buddies. Cut each strip in half, so the lengths are at least 20".

Cut 4 strips 1½" wide of each of the 6 pink bargello buddies. Cut each strip in half, so the lengths are at least 20".

Sew into 3 green and 7 pink strip-sets. Press the seams open. Cut into segments.

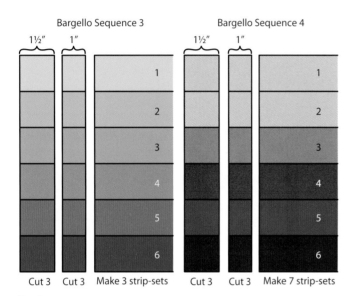

Fig. 4

For each bargello 3 sequence, cut the segments as follows (fig. 4):
3 segments 1½" (total 18)
3 segments 1" (total 18)

For each bargello sequence 4, cut the segments as follows (fig. 4):
3 segments 1½" (total 54)
3 segments 1" (total 54)

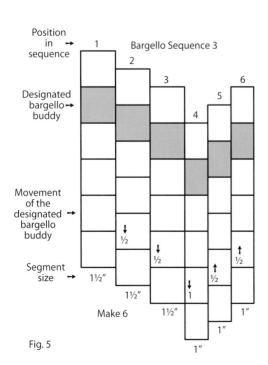

Fig. 5

Bargello sequence 1

Bargello sequence 2

Make 2

Make 6

Fig. 3

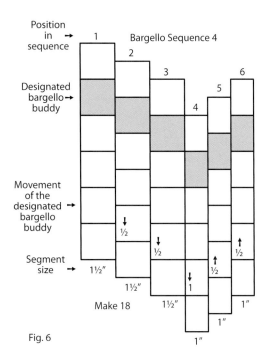

Position in sequence →

Bargello Sequence 4

1 2 3 4 5 6

Designated bargello → buddy

Movement of the designated → bargello buddy

Segment size →   1½"   1½"   1½"   1½"   1"   1"

½ ½ 1 ½ ½

1" 1"

Make 18

Fig. 6

Arrange the segments for each sequence as shown in figure 5, page 40, and figure 6.

Sew the segments together. Press the seams open.

Make bargello strips by sewing 6 sequences together, positioning the first segment of the next sequence one step up from the sixth segment of the preceding sequence (fig. 7, page 43). Press the seams open.

Trim all the bargello strips to measure 4" wide as shown in figure 8.

Diamond Assembly

Cut 4 strips 4" x 28" of both the brown and green straight fabrics (total 8).

Cut 8 strips 4" x 28" of the turquoise straight fabrics.

Sew the bargello and straight fabric strips into 4 different sets, 2 of each set, offsetting each strip by 4" as shown (fig. 9):

Set A—turquoise bargello, pink bargello, brown straight, brown bargello

Set B—turquoise bargello, turquoise straight, pink bargello, brown straight

Set C—green straight, turquoise bargello, turquoise straight, pink bargello

Set D—green bargello, green straight, turquoise bargello, turquoise straight

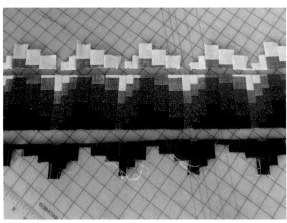

Fig. 8

Fig. 9

Bargello Sequence 3

Bargello Sequence 4

Make 1

Make 3

Fig. 7

Fig. 10

Fig. 11

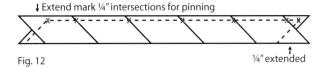

↓ Extend mark ¼" intersections for pinning

Fig. 12   ¼" extended

Align the 45-degree line on a rotary ruler with the top edge of the set. Trim along the side of the ruler. From the edge just cut, measure 4" and cut again (fig. 10). There's your first strip for a diamond! From each set, cut 4 strips. Label them with the set letter.

Use chalk to make X registration marks at both ends of each bargello strip and each intersection to indicate the ¼" seam allowance.

Make 8 diamonds by sewing together a 4" strip from each set (A, B, C, and D), positioning the darker sides of the bargello as shown (fig. 11).

Align the registration marks and sew 4 strips together into a diamond. There'll be a ¼" overhang at each end of the strips (fig. 12).

Designer's Note: Pin!! These are bias edges and you don't want them to stretch or shift.

Press the seams open. Use spray starch to "block" the diamonds so they're all the same size.

Measure across the ends of the diamonds as shown in figure 13 (page 45) to determine the size of your setting squares and triangles. It should be 22½" but work with the measurement you have!

Designer's Note: The first time I made this quilt, I found my measurements were not all the same. Now is the time to figure that out and either take in a seam or let one out. These directions give the exact measurements for your setting squares and triangles. I prefer to cut mine slightly larger and square up at the end. So if you'd like to do that as well, add an inch to your measurement.

Cut 4 setting squares 22½" x 22½" from background fabric, and for the setting triangles, cut a square 31⅞" x 31⅞" twice on the diagonal (fig. 14).

On the reverse side of the diamonds, use chalk to mark Xs to indicate the ¼" seam allowance crossovers at each corner. On the reverse side of the setting squares and triangles, mark Xs to indicate the ¼" seam allowance (fig. 15).

Assemble the star into 4 sections, each one made up of 2 diamonds and one setting triangle. All the seams will be sewn towards the point where the 3 units meet. Use a scant ¼" seam allowance to accommodate the bulk of the bargello.

Starting at the outside edge of a diamond and setting triangles, match the X marks and sew from the outside edge to the inside X as shown (fig. 16, page 46).

Press the seams towards the setting triangles and press the seam between the diamonds open.

Designer's Note: Spray starch helps here!

Join the 4 sections in pairs and add a corner setting square in the same way the setting triangles were added.

Join the halves and add the last 2 corner setting squares as shown in the quilt top assembly diagram (page 47). Press as before.

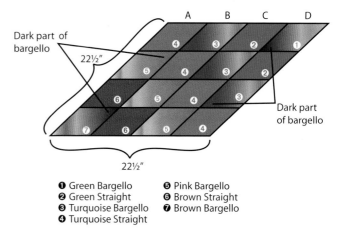

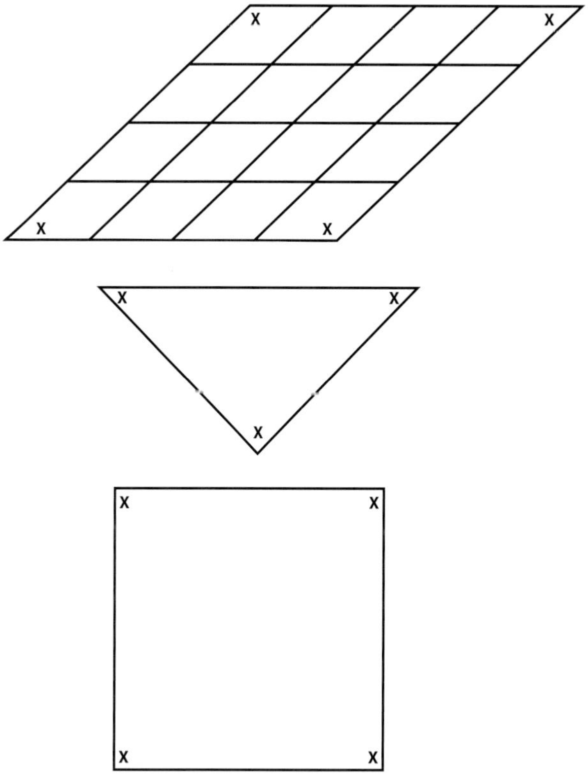

❶ Green Bargello ❺ Pink Bargello
❷ Green Straight ❻ Brown Straight
❸ Turquoise Bargello ❼ Brown Bargello
❹ Turquoise Straight

Fig. 13

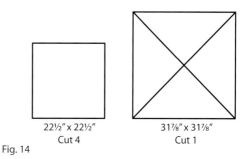

22½" x 22½"   31⅞" x 31⅞"
Cut 4   Cut 1

Fig. 14

Fig. 15

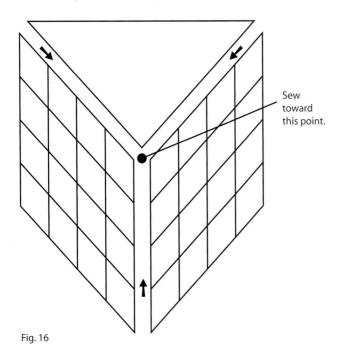

Sew toward this point.

Fig. 16

Borders

Cut 7 strips 5½" wide of border fabric. Sew end-to-end to make one long strip.

Cut 2 strips the length of the quilt and add to the sides.

Cut 2 strips the width of the quilt, including the side borders, and add to the top and bottom.

Quilt and bind as desired.

Appliqué

This quilt is appliquéd after it is quilted. The swirls (pages 48–49) are hand appliquéd with a needle-turn method. The leaf centers are reverse appliquéd with a decorative stitch and then, using the same decorative stitch, appliquéd (actually quilted) in place. There are 3 swirl motifs and 14 leaves used in each corner. The appliqué uses freezer-paper templates.

Designer's Note: Position the swirls slightly differently in each corner. The appliqué should overlap the star so it is tied into the design. Choose a variey of the lighter bargello buddies

for the leaf centers. Choose greens similar to the straight green fabric.

Swirl Appliqué

Trace the swirl motifs once onto freezer paper. Cut out freezer-paper templates on the traced lines. With a dry iron, press these templates onto the RIGHT side of the chosen fabric, leaving space between the templates for an ⅛"–¼" seam allowance.

Cut the fabric around the template, leaving approximately ⅛"–¼" seam allowance. Pin each piece in place on one corner of the quilt. Using a needle-turn method of appliqué and the freezer paper as a guide, sew into place. Remove the freezer-paper templates and repeat in each corner.

To make a single leaf, trace the leaf shape onto freezer paper. Cut out on the drawn line.

Trace the center shape onto the paper side of lightweight fusible web. Cut out the fusible web ¼" beyond the drawn line. (Remember when tracing onto fusible web, you need to trace in reverse.)

Press the freezer-paper template to the right of your leaf fabric. Cut out ¼" beyond the edge of the freezer paper.

Peel off the freezer-paper template. Place the leaf right-side down on an ironing surface. Fuse the web to the back of the leaf fabric following the manufacturer's instructions. Cut out the center of the leaf along the traced lines, leaving ¼" of fusible web around the cut-out center in the leaf fabric.

Fuse the cut-out leaf to a light bargello buddy fabric, with both facing right-side up. Cut away from the bargello buddy fabric. Place stabilizer beneath the leaf and appliqué the center to the leaf using a decorative stitch. Trim the excess center fabric and stabilizer.

Place the leaf right-side down onto a piece of lightweight interfacing. Using a small straight stitch, sew around the leaf. Trim the seam allowance. Cut a slit in the back of the interfacing

and turn the leaf right-side out. Press with a steam iron to flatten.

Repeat this process to make 56 leaves.

Arrange the leaves around the swirls on the quilt, grouping same-color center leaves together. Use the same decorative stitch to appliqué the leaves in place.

Quilt top assembly

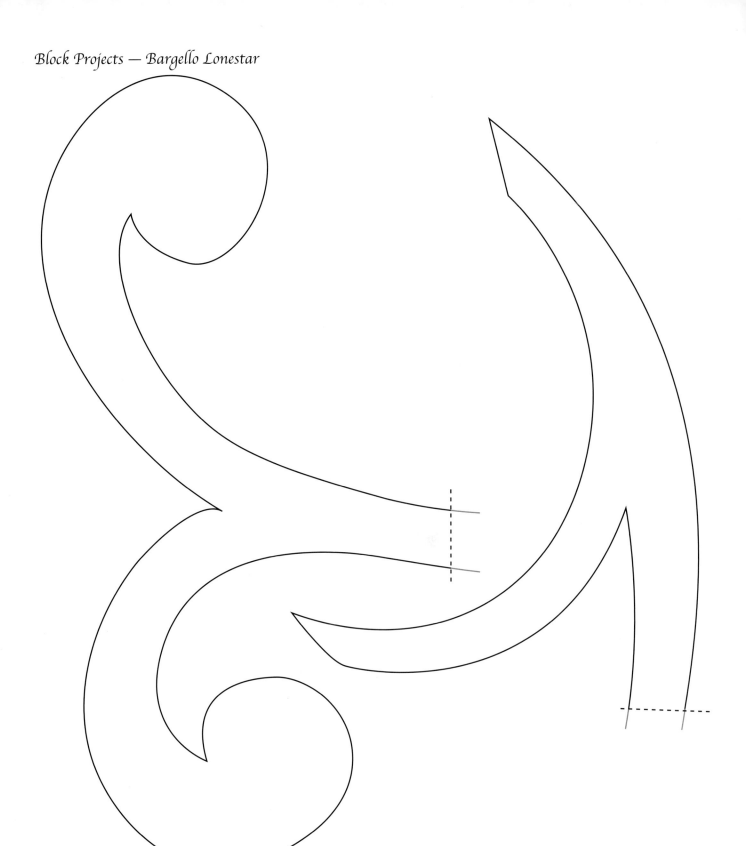

Pinwheels & Pyramids

79" x 89", made by the author

BITS *of* Bargello – Karen Gibbs

Fabrics & Supplies

You need 6 bargello buddies:

> ¾ yard of the darkest bargello buddy (bargello buddy 1)
>
> ⅝ yard each of 4 bargello buddies (bargello buddies 2–5)
>
> ⅜ yard of 1 bargello buddy (bargello buddy 6)

2½ yards feature straight fabric

1½ yards striped fabric for pinwheels and binding

3¼ yards secondary straight for pinwheels and inner border (a textured solid works well here)

2¼ yards neutral background for setting squares and triangles (Add ⅝ yard to replace one of the bargello buddies if you'd like to include the background fabric in your bargello sequences.)

6 yards backing

87" x 97" batting

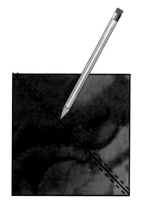

Make 12

Fig. 1

Pinwheel Blocks

Cut 6 squares 9½" x 9½" from both the striped fabric and the secondary straight fabric (12 total).

Make 12 half-square triangle units (fig. 1). Square up to measure 8½" x 8½".

Cut 12 squares 8½" x 8½" from the main straight fabric. Make 24 half-square triangle units with these squares and the striped half-square triangle units (fig. 2). Square up to measure 8" x 8".

Make 24

Fig. 2

Arrange the half-square triangle units into Pinwheel blocks as shown (fig. 3). Note that there will be 3 blocks with a striped center pinwheel and 3 blocks with the secondary straight fabric in the center.

Piecing the Bargello

Cut 14 strips 1¼" wide of bargello buddies #2, #3, #4, and #5 (56 total).

Cut 7 strips 1¼" wide of bargello buddies #1 and #6 (14 total).

Sew the bargello buddies into 7 strip-sets (fig. 4), mirroring the arrangement on either side of

bargello buddy #1. (Bargello buddies #1 and #6 are only used once in each strip-set.) Press the seams open.

For each bargello sequence, cut the segments as follows (fig. 4):
6 segments 1½" (72 total)
8 segments 1" (96 total)
7 segments ¾" (84 total)

Arrange the segment widths for each sequence as shown (fig. 5). Note that segments to the left of the center segment (position 1) mirror the arrangement of the segments to the right.

Make 3

Make 3

Fig. 3

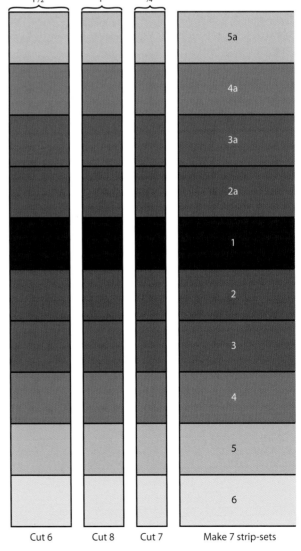

Cut 6   Cut 8   Cut 7   Make 7 strip-sets

Fig. 4

Loop all the pieces (fig. 6) with the exception of the segments in positions 1, 11, and 11a, sewing bargello buddy #5a to bargello buddy #6, right sides together. Finger press the seam open. Be careful to maintain the arrangement of the segments.

For positions 2 and 2a, remove the seam between bargello buddy #5 and #6.

For positions 3 and 3a, remove the seam between bargello buddy #4 and #5.

For positions 4 and 4a, remove the seam between bargello buddy #3 and #4.

For positions 5 and 5a remove the seam between bargello buddy #2 and #3.

Continue in this manner through positions 10 and 10a. Note that bargello buddy #5a looks to be "traveling" down a step each time (fig . 7).

Sew the segments together in pairs. Press the seams open. Sew the pairs together, starting

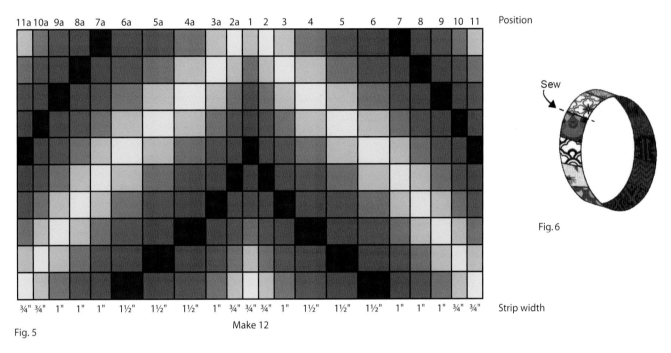

Fig. 5

Position (top of Fig. 5): 11a 10a 9a 8a 7a 6a 5a 4a 3a 2a 1 2 3 4 5 6 7 8 9 10 11

Strip width (bottom of Fig. 5): ¾" ¾" 1" 1" 1" 1½" 1½" 1½" 1" ¾" ¾" ¾" 1" 1½" 1½" 1½" 1" 1" 1" ¾" ¾"

Make 12

Sew

Fig. 6

Fig. 7

Position:	11a	10a	9a	8a	7a	6a	5a	4a	3a	2a	1	2	3	4	5	6	7	8	9	10	11
	5a	4a	3a	2a	1	2	3	4	5	6	5a	6	5	4	3	2	1	2a	3a	4a	5a
	4a	3a	2a	1	2	3	4	5	6	5a	4a	5a	6	5	4	3	2	1	2a	3a	4a
	3a	2a	1	2	3	4	5	6	5a	4a	3a	4a	5a	6	5	4	3	2	1	2a	3a
	2a	1	2	3	4	5	6	5a	4a	3a	2a	3a	4a	5a	6	5	4	3	2	1	2a
Fabric #:	1	2	3	4	5	6	5a	4a	3a	2a	1	2a	3a	4a	5a	6	5	4	3	2	1
	2	3	4	5	6	5a	4a	3a	2a	1	2	1	2a	3a	4a	5a	6	5	4	3	2
	3	4	5	6	5a	4a	3a	2a	1	2	3	2	1	2a	3a	4a	5a	6	5	4	3
	4	5	6	5a	4a	3a	2a	1	2	3	4	3	2	1	2a	3a	4a	5a	6	5	4
	5	6	5a	4a	3a	2a	1	2	3	4	5	4	3	2	1	2a	3a	4a	5a	6	5
	6	5a	4a	3a	2a	1	2	3	4	5	6	5	4	3	2	1	2a	3a	4a	5a	6a
Strip Width:	¾"	¾"	1"	1"	1"	1½"	1½"	1½"	1"	¾"	¾"	¾"	1"	1½"	1½"	1½"	1"	1"	1"	¾"	¾"

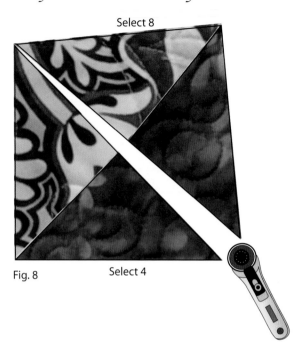

Select 8

Fig. 8   Select 4

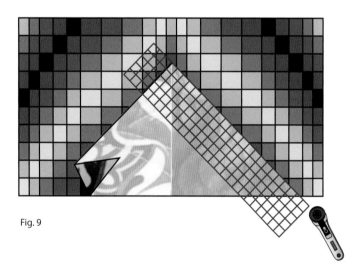

Fig. 9

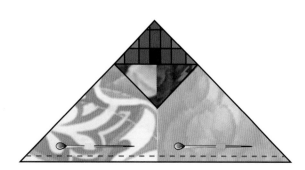

Fig. 10. Make 12

each seam at the opposite end of the segments to ensure your sequence will remain straight and not distort. Press the seams open. Continue until the sequence is complete.

Bargello Pinwheel Blocks

Cut 4 squares 9½" x 9½" from both the straight feature fabric and the secondary straight fabric (total 8). Make 8 half-square triangle units. Square up to measure 8½" x 8½".

Cut each half-square triangle unit in half on the diagonal, perpendicular to the center seam (fig. 8). Select 8 triangles with the feature fabric on the left and 4 triangles with the feature fabric on the right. (You'll have 4 triangles left over.)

Take a cut triangle and place it on a bargello sequence, right sides together. Line up the center point of the triangle with the center bargello strip (position 1). Using the triangle as a template, cut a bargello triangle to the same size (fig. 9).

DO NOT move the pieces you are cutting; rotate the ruler or use a rotating cutting mat. Picking up the bargello can distort it.

While still on the cutting mat, pin the long sides of the triangles together. Now pick up and sew a ¼" seam (fig. 10). Press the seam away from the bargello.

Trim the 12 bargello half-square triangles to measure 8" x 8".

Gently set aside the leftover bargello so as not to distort it. It will be used later for the pyramids.

Assemble 3 bargello Pinwheel blocks—2 with the secondary straight fabric in the center and one with the feature straight fabric in the center (fig. 11, page 55).

Piecing the Pyramids

Look carefully at the pyramids in the quilt photo (page 50). They are half-square triangle units too!

Cut 7 squares 7½" x 7½" from both the darkest bargello buddy fabric and the secondary straight fabric (14 total).

Make 14 half-square triangle units. Trim to measure 6½" x 6½".

Cut each half-square triangle unit in half on the diagonal, perpendicular to the center seam (refer to fig. 8, page 54).

Position 26 of the cut triangles on the leftover bargello pieces, right sides together. Cut bargello triangles to size as before, using the pieced triangles as templates (fig. 12, page 56).

Pin the triangles together, sew with a ¼" seam, and press the seam allowance toward the pieced triangle (fig. 13, page 56). Trim to measure 5½" x 5½".

Sew 2 rows of 13 matching pyramid units each as shown (fig. 14, page 56). Note that pyramids in the two rows will face in opposite directions. Always place the secondary straight fabric at the top. Press the seams away from the bargello.

Joining the Blocks

From the neutral background fabric, cut:
2 squares 23" x 23"
4 squares 15½" x 15½"
2 squares 12" x 12"

Cut the 23" squares twice on the diagonal for the 8 side-setting triangles.

Make 2

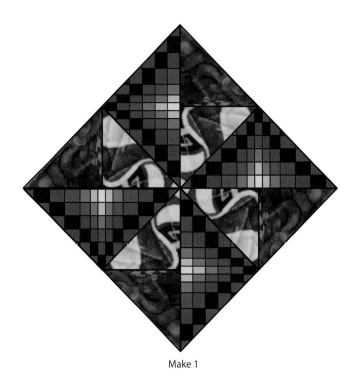

Make 1

Fig. 11

Cut the 12" squares once on the diagonal for the 4 corner triangles.

Designer's Note: The outside setting triangles are cut slightly larger than necessary to allow for discrepancies in sewing.

Assemble the blocks, setting squares, and triangles in diagonal rows. Trim the outside edges to a ¼" seam allowance from the points of the blocks.

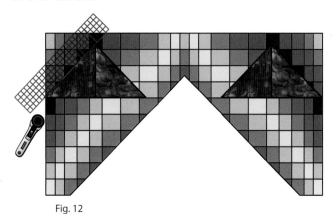

Fig. 12

Make 13

Fig. 13

Make 13

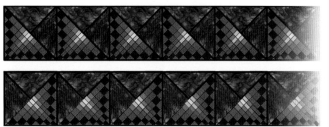

Fig. 14

Borders

Cut 4 strips 2½" wide of the secondary straight fabric. Sew end-to-end to make one long strip. Then cut 2 strips 65½" long and add to the lower edge of the pyramid rows.

Cut 4 strips 3" wide of the secondary straight fabric. Sew end-to-end to make one long strip. Then cut 2 strips 65½" long and add to the top edge of the pyramid rows.

Add the pyramid borders to the top and bottom of the quilt. Make sure both rows of pyramids are oriented correctly (refer to the quilt top assembly on page 57).

Designer's Note: The slight variation in these strip sizes helps ground the pyramids, but still allows them to float in the border and stand out. Pointing both rows of pyramids made the most sense to me. They don't look like pyramids if they're pointing down.

Cut 5 strips 5¼" wide of the secondary straight fabric. Sew end-to-end to make one long strip. Then cut 2 strips 84½" long (or the length measurement of your quilt) and add to the sides.

Cut 8 strips 4" wide of the main straight fabric. Sew end-to-end to make one long strip. Measure the width of your quilt; cut strips to that measurement, and add to the top and bottom of the quilt. Measure the length of your quilt and in the same manner, add to the sides of the quilt.

Designer's Note: I chose to do a wider inner border. I felt a wider border of the feature straight fabric would overpower the quilt.

Quilt top assembly

Musically Speaking

69" x 72", made by the author

I wanted to do a music quilt that was a little unconventional. I used reverse appliqué for the bargello notes to give them a 3-D effect and a different bargello sequence for the flags to provide movement. I chose a white background with black lines for the staff, then color for the notes.

Choose your favorite colorway or go with school colors, which usually have high contrast. For consistency, use the same colorway for the four-patch sashing and the music staff.

While making this quilt, one of my little ones was picking out a holiday tune on the piano, in mid-summer! This quilt works well with holiday fabric, too, and it's available most places by June. This quilt is a great stashbuster.

Fabrics & Supplies

1¼ yard dark fabric for music staff and four-patch sashing

1½ yards light background fabric

½ yard of 6 bargello buddies or 12 fat quarters (3 yards total)

¼ yard of 6 fabrics for four-patch blocks (1½ yards total)

¼ yard for setting strips

¼ yard of 6–8 fabrics for piano key border 1½–2 yards total)

½ yard for border and additional piano keys

4¾ yards backing

⅝ yard binding

77" x 80" batting

freezer paper

stabilizer

matching thread

Music Staff Background

Cut 8 rectangles 12½" x 18½" of background fabric (fig. 1).

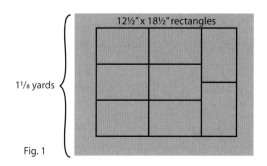

12½" x 18½" rectangles

1⅛ yards

Fig. 1

Cut 40 bias strips 1" wide and at least 22" long. Fold in both long edges ¼" to make ½" wide bias strips. Press.

Designer's Note: I never like to fold over the edges of bias strips. I prefer to go to my ironing board and weave a pin through the cover, making a ½" space in the middle of the pin to feed the bias through. With the bias strip right-side down, I fold the raw edges in to meet in the center and feed the strip under the pin. As I pull the bias through, it folds itself (fig. 2). I press as I go.

Weave a pin in your ironing board cover

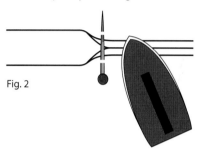

Fig. 2

Arrange 5 bias strips on each background rectangle (fig. 3). Space the strips equally as in written music or arrange them starting closer together on one side, spreading out as they cross the block—kind of like going from *pp* to *ff*.

Fig. 3

Pin in place. Stitch the bias strips to the background with a straight stitch along both edges. Use matching thread or spice it up a bit with a decorative stitch.

Designer's Note: I tried to make each of these blocks different—in the way I placed the staff as well as the way I placed the notes. I also varied the notes by using different bargello buddies.

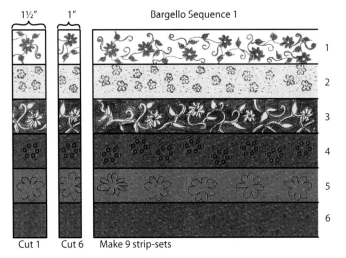

Fig. 4

Cut 1   Cut 6   Make 9 strip-sets

Bargello Sequence 1

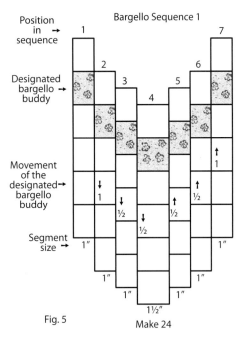

Fig. 5   Make 24

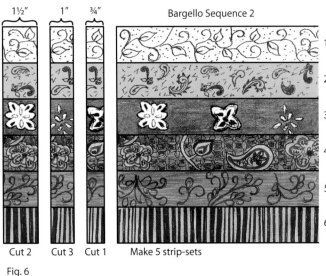

Cut 2   Cut 3   Cut 1   Make 5 strip-sets

Fig. 6

Bargello Sequence 2

Piecing the Bargello

There are 3 bargello sequences in this quilt. Sequence 1 for the notes, sequence 2 for the flags on the notes, and sequence 3 for the beams (the flags joining two notes). The bargello buddy strips are cut the same width for all three sequences, so you can mix them up and use all three sequences in all three places like I did.

Cut each bargello buddy into 9 strips 1¼" wide. Cut each strip in half, so the lengths are at least 20".

Determine the layout of your bargello buddies for all three sequences and make a key for each.

You'll make a total of 17 strip-sets, varying the arrangement and fabrics, keeping the darkest bargello buddy at the bottom of each strip-set to give the illusion of shadowing.

Bargello Sequence 1 for the Notes

For each note bargello sequence, cut the segments as follows (fig. 4):

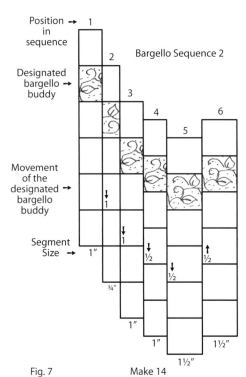

Fig. 7   Make 14

1 segment 1½" (24 total)
6 segments 1" (144 total)

Arrange the segments for each sequence as shown (fig. 5).

Sew the segments together. Press the seams open.

Bargello Sequence 2 for the Flags

For each note flag bargello sequence, cut the segments as follows (fig. 6):
2 segments 1½" (28 total)
3 segments 1" (42 total)
1 segment ¾" (14 total)

Arrange the segments for each sequence as shown (fig. 7).

Sew the segments together. Press the seams open.

Bargello Sequence 3 for the Beams

For each note beam (the flag joining two notes) cut the segments as follows (fig. 8):
2 segments 1½" (10 total)
6 segments 1" (30 total)
1 segment ¾" (5 total)

Arrange the segments for each sequence as shown (fig. 9).

Sew the segments together. Press the seams open.

Appliquéing the Notes

Using the full-size templates (page 65) make a placement guide by tracing three styles of notes onto clear plastic—one note with the stem up, one with the stem down, and two joined notes (fig. 10). Notice that when the stem is up, the flag shape is different than when the stem is down.

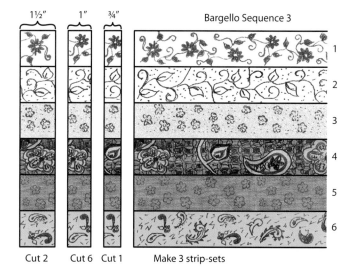

Fig. 8

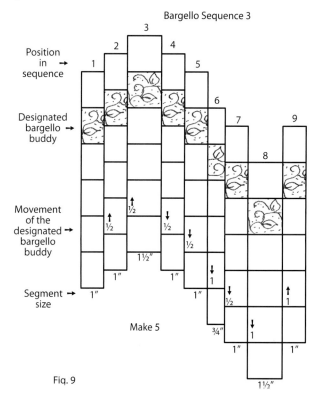

Fig. 9

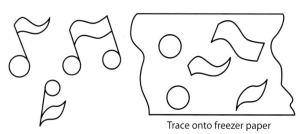

Trace onto freezer paper

Fig. 10

Fig. 11

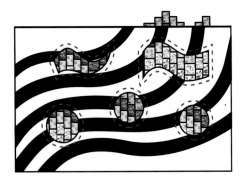

Fig. 12

 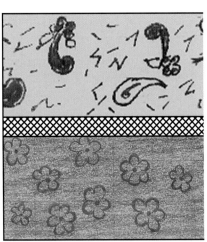

6"

Cut 16   Make 6 strip-sets

Fig. 13

Designer's Note: The notes are obviously bigger than what would be on the music staffs you've made. Stretch your artistic license a little further and make your notes a little jaunty—tilting them on a slight angle.

Trace the full-size oval, flags, and beam patterns (page 65) onto freezer paper. Cut out on the drawn line. Position freezer-paper templates onto the music staffs of the background blocks, using the placement guide to position them properly. Press into place.

Staystitch around each shape (fig. 11). Peel off the templates and re-use. Carefully cut out the background inside the staystitching. Cut smoothly, as this will be the guide you will use for the machine appliqué.

Designer's Note: I like to staystitch with a contrasting thread and a little bit larger stitch so I can actually see where I'm supposed to cut!

Position the appropriate bargello sequence behind the cutouts (fig. 12). Pin in place. Position stabilizer beneath the bargello and machine appliqué in place. Trim the excess stabilizer and bargello.

Trace the note stem onto freezer paper. Cut out on the drawn line. Press the stem template to the right side of the fabric. Cut out the stem leaving ⅛"–¼" around the template. Using a needle-turn hand appliqué method and the freezer paper as a guide, appliqué into place. Peel off the template and reuse for the remaining note stems. Trace additional templates as needed.

Four-Patch Block Assembly

Cut your remaining bargello buddy fabrics into 6" x 18½" strips.

Cut dark fabric strips 1½" x 18½".

Make 6 strip-sets as shown. Cut into 16 segments 6" wide (fig. 13).

Chain stitch 8 segments onto 1½" wide strips of dark fabric as shown (fig. 14). Trim and press toward the narrow strips.

Join with the remaining 6" segments, aligning the dark sashing strip between the squares (fig. 15).

The finished four-patch units should measure 12½" x 12½".

Quilt Assembly
Cut 4 setting strips 3½" x 12½".

Arrange the blocks with the setting strips at alternate ends of the rows as shown in the quilt top assembly (page 64).

Borders
Cut 18 rectangles 7½" x 12½" from the border fabrics. Make 2 rows of 9 rectangles each (see page 64). Press the seams open. Add to the top and bottom of the quilt top.

Cut 4 strips 3½" wide of border fabric. Join in pairs end-to-end and cut strips 72½" long. Sew to the sides of the quilt. Press the seams toward the border.

Quilting
Prior to quilting, press the bargello segments with spray starch.

Try a spiral of quilting in the notes to accent the shape. In the flags and beams of the notes, follow the bargello shape with undulating quilting lines. Echo the music lines close to the bias strips, then use an allover design of small notes and loops with matching thread in the background. The piano key border looks nice with an orange peel effect on each seam or try enlarging the allover music and loops design with a contrasting thread.

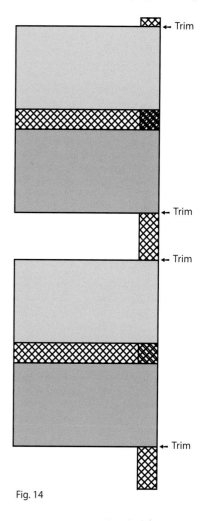

Fig. 14

Make 8

Fig. 15

Quilt top assembly

Radiating Dresden Plates

55" x 70", made by the author

This quilt plays with a circle of bargello using wedges, but only ¼ of the circle at a time. I pulled my favorite color combination from my straight fabric and chose textured solids and batiks for my bargello buddies. I used more color variation in the plates, adding green for contrast.

The chaos in this quilt comes from the Dresden Plates. Have fun shopping for fat quarters that go with your straight fabric. The more the merrier.

Fabrics & Supplies

12 fat quarters in varying prints for the plate blades and pieced border
1 fat quarter each of 5 bargello buddies in graduated shades
2½ yards straight fabric for background
¾ yard for inner border and binding
4⅝ yards for backing
63" x 78" batting
freezer paper for a 10" circle template
matching thread for machine appliqué
spray starch
stabilizer
appliqué scissors

Piecing the Bargello

Determine the layout of your bargello buddies and make a key, numbered #1 through #5.

Cut 11 strips 1½" wide x 22" from each bargello buddy fat quarter perpendicular to the selvage.

Make 11 strip-sets as shown in figure 1, alternating the direction you sew the strips. Press the seams open.

For each bargello sequence, cut the segments as follows (fig. 1).
3 segments 1¾" (total of 48)
2 segments 1½" (total of 32)
4 segments 1¼" (total of 64)

Loop all the pieces with the exception of position 1, sewing bargello buddy #5 to bargello buddy #1, right sides together. Finger press the seam open.

Sew

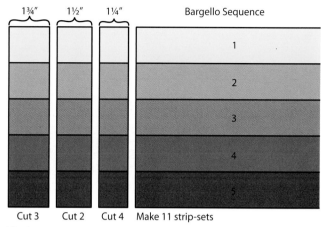

	1¾"	1½"	1¼"		Bargello Sequence
Cut 3	Cut 2	Cut 4		Make 11 strip-sets	

Fig. 1

In this bargello sequence position 1 is in the middle, 2–5 are on the right, 2a–5a are on the left. Arrange the widths as shown in figure 2.

For positions 2 and 2a, remove the seam between bargello buddy #1 and #2.

For positions 3 and 3a, remove the seam between bargello buddy #2 and #3.

For positions 4 and 4a remove the seam between bargello buddy #3 and #4.

For position 5 and 5a, remove the seam between bargello buddy #4 and #5.

Position:	5a	4a	3a	2a	1	2	3	4	5
	4	3	2	1	5	1	2	3	4
	3	2	1	5	4	5	1	2	3
Fabric #:	2	1	5	4	3	4	5	1	2
	1	5	4	3	2	3	4	5	1
	5	4	3	2	1	2	3	4	5
Strip Width:	1¾"	1¼"	1¼"	1½"	1¾"	1½"	1¼"	1¼"	1¾"

Fig. 2

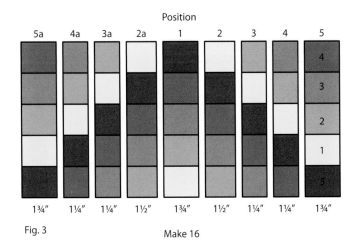

Position

5a	4a	3a	2a	1	2	3	4	5

| 1¾" | 1¼" | 1¼" | 1½" | 1¾" | 1½" | 1¼" | 1¼" | 1¾" |

Fig. 3   Make 16

The sequence will now look like this (fig. 3).

Prior to sewing the segments together, you need to wedge-cut them to get the fan effect.

Find the center ½" at the bottom of each segment by folding it in half, pinching in a crease, and marking ¼" on either side with chalk or colored pencil.

Line up a ruler from the left mark to the upper left corner of the segment and trim.

Line up a ruler from the right mark to the upper right corner of the segment and trim (fig. 4).

Starting with position 1, sew the wedges together using a scant ¼" seam allowance, matching the seam between the top two bargello buddies, and sewing from top to bottom with the exception of adding 3 and 3a; sew from the bottom up on those seams.

Piece the entire bargello unit before pressing the seams to one side (not open this time!). Make 16 (fig. 5).

Making the Dresden Plates

There are 6 plate blades in each block and 16 blocks in the basic quilt.

Cut 8 rectangles 3" x 9½" from each of the 12 plate blade fat quarters (total of 96).

Place all the rectangles into 3–4 piles according to their colors. Pull one from every pile and double up on some of the piles so you have groups of 6 rectangles.

Designer's Note: We are going for a controlled chaos, so this quilt may look scrappy, but each

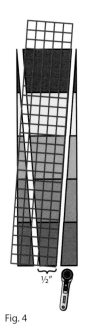

½"

Fig. 4

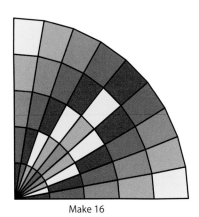

Make 16

Fig. 5

plate has one wedge from each pile and a second from at least one of the piles.

Fan out the rectangles and move them around until you get an arrangement pleasing to your eye. The plates are not supposed to be all matching!

Repeat the process for all 16 blocks.

Fold each plate blade rectangle in half lengthwise, right sides together. Sew a ¼" seam across one end of the rectangle. Trim the seam at an angle as shown (fig. 6).

Finger press the seam to one side, turn the point right-side out, and press. The seam should fall directly in the center of the strip.

Designer's Note: Slide the corner of a rotary ruler up into the point of the triangle formed by the seam until the 2" marks line up with the edges of the triangle, forcing it to lie flat. Then slowing remove the ruler as you press, starting at the point. This helps the seam to fall evenly.

Wedge-cut the plate blades in the same way as you trimmed the bargello segments (fig. 7).

Trim only the inside edge of the two outermost blades on each plate (fig. 8).

Sew the 6 blades (4 trimmed on both sides, and one each trimmed on one side) together for each plate, aligning the bottom corners of the triangle point at the top of the blades. Press the seams to one side.

Block Assembly
Cut 16 squares 12½" x 12½" of background fabric.

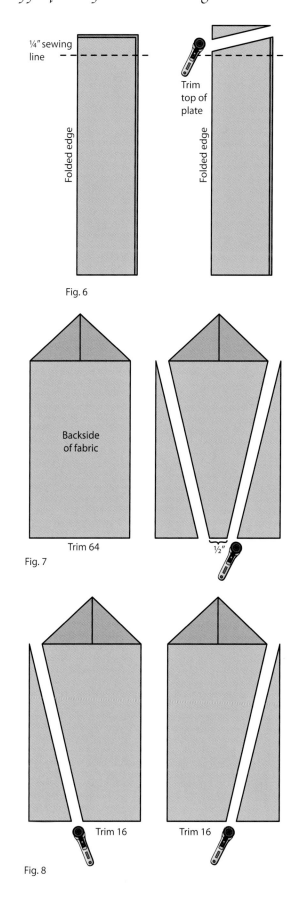

¼" sewing line

Trim top of plate

Folded edge

Folded edge

Fig. 6

Backside of fabric

Trim 64

Fig. 7

½"

Trim 16

Trim 16

Fig. 8

Fig. 9

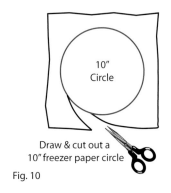

Draw & cut out a
10" freezer paper circle

Fig. 10

Fold circle
in half twice

Fig. 11

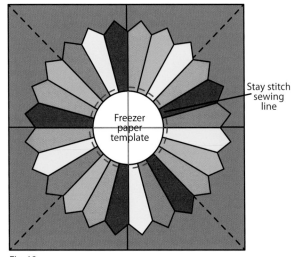

Fig. 12

Lay the center 4 squares together. If you have a directional print for your background now is the time to note that! Lay 4 plates at the center of these squares. Position the plates so the outside edges of the points align with the edges of the block (fig. 9).

The center seam of the plates should be at a 45-degree angle to the sides of the blocks and the points of the outermost blades about 1" from the unfinished edge of the block. Don't worry about the outside blades overhanging the edge of the block—this is fudge room.

You want the 4 plates to line up to form a continuous circle. If one is off a little, pull it out and try one of the other plates, saving the pulled one for a place all by itself! Stand back and look at the color placement. If you have a strong color in one of the plates, you probably want it to appear in each of the quadrants, for balance.

Draw and cut out a 10" circle of freezer paper (fig. 10).

Designer's Note: I used my favorite mixing bowl as opposed to trying to find a compass or template.

Fold the circle in half twice (fig. 11), then unfold.

Butt the edges of the blocks together and line up the folds of the circle with the edges of the 4 blocks. Trace a line around the circle, marking the plates. Remove the plates from the background and staystitch on that line to stabilize (fig. 12). Cut the plates just inside the staystitching in a smooth curve.

Position the bargello units in the corners of the blocks. The top of the bargello wedge will fall inside the ¼" seam allowance but not be all the way to the edge of the block. The bottom of this wedge will overlap the bottom corner of the 12½" square. Lay the plates on the background squares to overlap the bargello a little bit. Pin well or baste.

Position stabilizer under the blocks. Appliqué the plate blades to the background and to the bargello bits using a narrow zigzag or buttonhole stitch (fig. 13).

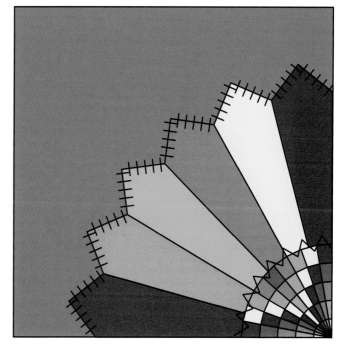

Fig. 13

Flip the block over and trim away the excess bargello that overhangs the edge of the block. Using appliqué scissors, trim away the background fabric from behind the plates. Join the 4 blocks together to form the center unit as shown in the photo on page 72.

In the same way, position and trim the double plates for the sides and single plates for the corners. Sew 4 double-plate units as shown in the quilt top assembly (page 73).

Designer's Note: Appliqué scissors are worth their weight in gold. I chose to trim away the excess background fabric because I used a rather distinctive print and it shows through the plates. Also, I remove the stabilizer, even though you don't have to. Coming from a longarm perspective, the less bulk the better.

Quilt Assembly

Sew the units and remaining blocks into rows and sew the rows together as shown on page 17. Remove any basting.

Cut 48 rectangles 2½" x 4¾" from the remaining fat quarters. Sew into rows of 24 for the "piano key" borders. Press the seams open.

Add the piano key borders to the top and bottom of the quilt. Press the seams toward the quilt.

Cut 6 strips 1¼" wide of the red inner border fabric. Add to the quilt (see Adding Borders, page 9).

Cut the remaining straight fabric into 6 strips 3½" wide. Add to the quilt.

Quilting Your Quilt

This quilt radiates out from the center. I wanted to add a sense of movement to it so I chose to do an undulating swirl vine radiating out from each Dresden Plate with thread that blended with the background fabric. I did clamshells in the bargello with yellow thread. The plates are anchored with stitching in the ditch. There's a simple swirl in the borders, scaled to their width, and an undulating vine done with variegated thread on the piano keys.

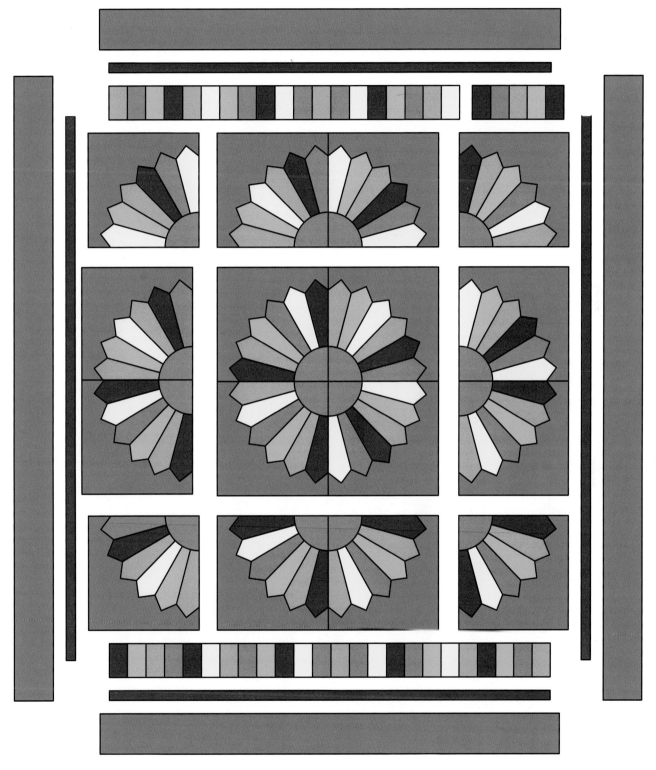

Quilt top assembly

Gone Fishing

61" x 66", made by the author

This quilt is designed for all those fishing fanatics out there. To me, this is a worthy hobby—it gives me time to quilt while my husband takes the kids and spends endless hours in the fresh air doing who knows what!

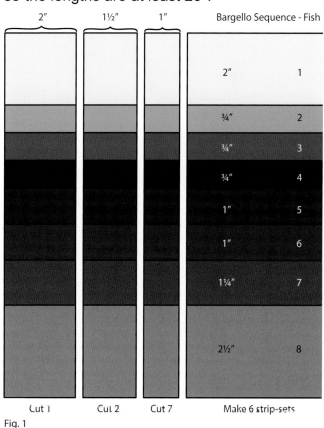

I started this design with a straight fabric and picked fat quarters to go with it. The secondary straight fabric I picked for the 6" x 6" squares didn't work with the fat quarters, so I used a marbleized fabric from my stash. It has the movement of water and certain areas of it can be perceived as fish scales (note some of the appliqué!).

Be careful not to blend your bargello buddies too much.

Fabrics & Supplies

¼ yard of 8 bargello buddies in browns and
    greens (for the fish)
¼ yard of 7 bargello buddies in blues and
    greens (for the water)
¾ yard main straight
½ yard (2) marbleized
    secondary straights (6½" squares)
1¾ yards total mixed fabrics
    (for the four-patch units)
½ yard water fabric
½ yard total of 2 light fabrics
    (for the sky backgrounds)
assorted scraps for fish appliqué
beads or sequins for eyes
matching thread for machine appliqué
stabilizer
freezer paper
½ yard inner border
4½ yards backing
½ yard binding

Bargello Fish Block Assembly
Making the Fish Bargello

This bargello sequence has smaller pieces at the top. When arranging your bargello buddies, have your darkest buddy in position #4, graduating to the lightest shades at the top and bottom of your strip-set. This will help with the 3-D effect we are going for. The top and bottom

buddies are more or less fillers and should be similar in value.

For the tail area of the fish, the bargello segments are cut into wedges to get the dramatic shape. The head and fins are hand appliquéd.

Determine the layout of your bargello buddies and make a key.

Cut 3 strips from each bargello buddy in the widths indicated (fig. 1). Cut each strip in half, so the lengths are at least 20".

Fig. 1

Make 6 strip-sets as shown, alternating the direction you sew the seams. Press the seams open.

For each bargello fish sequence, cut the segments as follows (fig. 1 above):
1 segment 2" (6 total)
2 segments 1½" (12 total)
7 segments 1" (42 total)

½"

Fig. 2

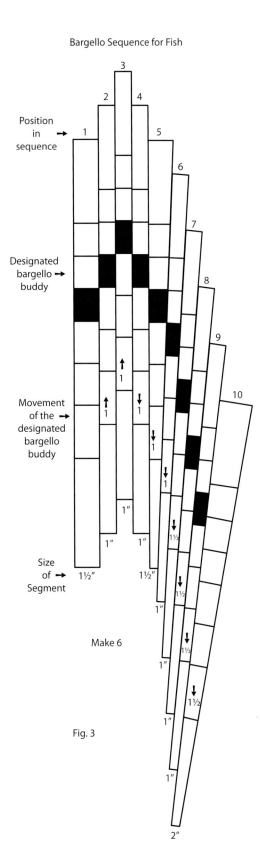

Bargello Sequence for Fish

Position in sequence →

Designated bargello buddy →

Movement of the designated bargello buddy →

Size of Segment →

Make 6

Fig. 3

Wedge-cut 6 of these segments for each fish.
1 segment 2"
1 segment 1½"
4 segments 1"

To wedge-cut a segment, fold it in half and pinch press the fold at the base of the segment. Mark ¼" on either side of the fold. Align a rotary ruler with the left-hand mark and the upper left corner of the segment and trim. In the same way, trim the right side (fig. 2).

Sew the segments and wedges in the sequence as shown (fig. 3). The offset steps are determined by the location of bargello buddy #4. Make 6 fish bargello sequences. Press the seams to one side.

Making the Background

Cut 6 rectangles 6½" x 12½" from the water fabric and 6 rectangles 6½" x 12½" from one of the sky fabrics (total of 12 rectangles).

Mark a line 2" from the top 12½" edge of a water fabric rectangle with chalk. Make a hill-and-valley cut (a sine curve) below the line with a rotary cutter (fig. 4, page 77).

Lay the curved water fabric onto a sky rectangle so the curve overlaps the sky fabric. Baste in place (fig. 5, page 77).

Designer's Note: If you like more control, or want uniformity, draw a curve on a 6½" x 12½" rectangle of freezer paper. Cut on the drawn line and press the freezer-paper template onto the water fabric rectangle. Following the template, cut the curve.

Enlarge and trace the body of the bargello fish pattern (page 81) onto freezer paper, marking where the head joins the body. Cut out along the drawn line.

Iron the freezer-paper template of the body onto the basted background, positioning your fish to look energetic and jumping. Staystitch around the template (fig. 6). Remove the freezer paper.

Place stabilizer beneath the block and machine appliqué the basted curve (between the sky and water), from both outside edges to the staystitching around the fish (fig. 7). Remove the basting and excess stabilizer.

Cut out the fish shape inside the staystitching. Position the bargello sequence behind the background, making sure the #4 buddy appears all the way across the fish (fig. 8).

Place stabilizer beneath the block and machine appliqué the fish. Trim the excess stabilizer and bargello from the back of the block.

Trace the fish head and fins onto freezer paper. Cut out on the drawn line. Use the templates to cut out the head and fins and hand appliqué them onto the bargello body. Add a bead for the eye of the fish.

Square up the blocks to measure 6½" x 12½".

Bargello Water Block Assembly
Making the Bargello Background
Light reflects off the top of water so you will want to have the lighter bargello buddies at the top of your strip-set for the water sequence.

Select 7 bargello buddies. If you have a favorite bargello buddy, make sure it is in the middle of the strip-set, because the top and bottom buddies will appear less often in this sequence.

Determine the layout of your bargello buddies and make a key.

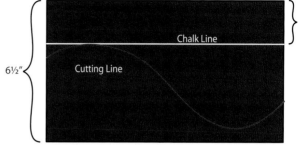
Water Fabric

Fig. 4

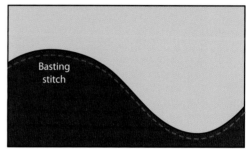

Fig. 5

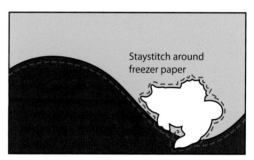

Fig. 6

Fig. 7

Fig. 8

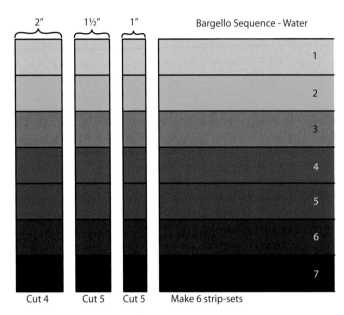

2"   1½"   1"

Bargello Sequence - Water

1
2
3
4
5
6
7

Cut 4   Cut 5   Cut 5   Make 6 strip-sets

Fig. 9

Cut 3 strips 1" wide from each bargello buddy fabric. Cut each strip in half, so the lengths are at least 20½".

Assemble 6 identical strip-sets, alternating the direction you sew the seams. Press the seams open.

For each water bargello sequence, cut the segments as follows (fig. 9):
4 segments 2" (24 total)
5 segments 1½" (30 total)
5 segments 1" (30 total)

Sew the segments in sequence as shown (fig. 10). The offset steps are determined by the location of bargello buddy #2. Make 6 water bargello sequences. Press the seams open.

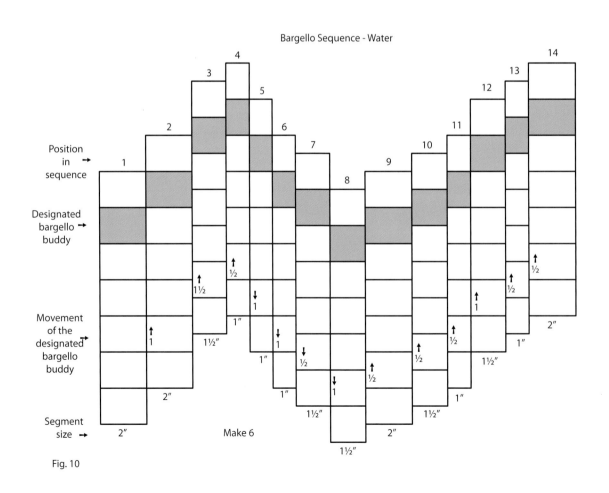

Bargello Sequence - Water

Fig. 10

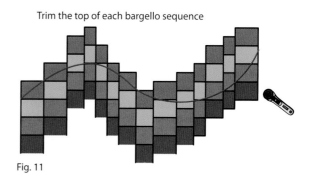

Use a rotary cutter to trim the bargello along the curve established by the segment positions (fig. 11).

Trim the top of each bargello sequence

Fig. 11

Designer's Note: Optionally, make your own curve shape, sew your strip-set, and cut varying widths of segments. Draw out a curve on a piece of paper and lay out the segments along the curve, overlapping the seam allowances and alternating the varying widths. Sew the segments together and trim.

Cut 6 rectangles 6½" x 12½" from the remaining sky fabric.

Lay the water bargello units onto the sky rectangles and baste together as before.

Appliquéing the Fish

Enlarge and trace the small fish pattern (page 81) onto clear plastic or X-ray film to use as a placement guide.

Enlarge and transfer the small fish pattern onto freezer paper. Cut out along the outside lines. Press the template on the background piece. Make sure your fish is enthusiastic and jumping (fig. 12). Draw a chalk line around the fish and peel off the freezer paper.

Machine appliqué the basted curve from both outside edges to the chalk line.

Cut apart the freezer-paper fish pattern. Make a separate piece for the fin on the body. Use the freezer paper to cut out the individual pieces for each fish. Appliqué the top and bottom portions of the fish together first. Add the head and fins. Then appliqué the completed fish to the background (see Appliqué Techniques, page 8). Add a bead for the eye of the fish.

Square up the blocks to measure 6½" x 12½".

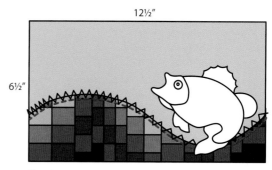

12½"

6½"

Fig. 12

Four-Patch Assembly

Cut four-patch fabrics into short strips 3½" x 11".

Arrange the strips into two piles with two different sets of color in each.

Designer's Note: I arranged all my yellows, oranges, and browns in pile #1 and all the greens and blues in pile #2. Each four-patch was made with two fabrics from each pile. This gives the look of random piecing, but it's controlled a little.

Make 36 small strip-sets with a strip from each pile (fig. 13, page 80).

Press the seams toward the fabric from pile #2. Cut 3 segments from each strip-set 3½" wide (you need a total of 104).

Four-patch assembly

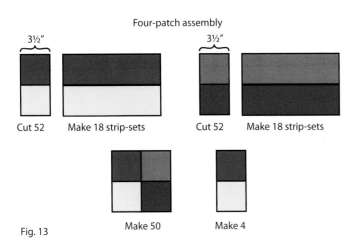

3½"   3½"

Cut 52   Make 18 strip-sets   Cut 52   Make 18 strip-sets

Fig. 13   Make 50   Make 4

Randomly select two segments and sew together, placing the color #2 fabrics in opposite corners, opposing the seam allowances. Four-patch units should measure 6½" x 6½".

You need 50 complete four-patch units for the blocks and borders and 4 additional two-patch segments for the borders.

Combined Block Assembly

Cut 12 rectangles 6½" x 12½" of your main straight fabric. If the fabric is directional, keep in mind that these rectangles will be used in a portrait orientation.

Cut 12 squares 6½" x 6½" of your secondary straight fabric.

Assemble 12 blocks as shown (fig. 14).

Quilt Assembly

Arrange the blocks as shown in the quilt top assembly. Join the blocks into rows and sew the rows together.

Borders

Cut the inner border fabric into seven 2" strips. Sew end-to-end to make one long strip. Measure the length of the quilt. Cut 2 strips that length and add to the sides of quilt. Measure the width of the quilt including the side borders. Cut 2 strips that length and add to the top and bottom.

Make 2 borders of 9 four-patch units and 1 two-patch segment. Add to the sides of the quilt.

Make 2 borders of 10 four-patch units and 1 two-patch segment. Add to the top and bottom of the quilt.

Quilt and bind as desired.

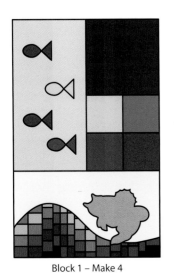

Block 1 – Make 4

Block 2 – Make 4

Block 3 – Make 2

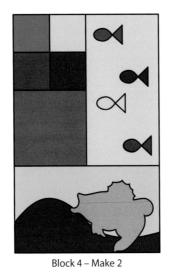

Block 4 – Make 2

Fig. 14

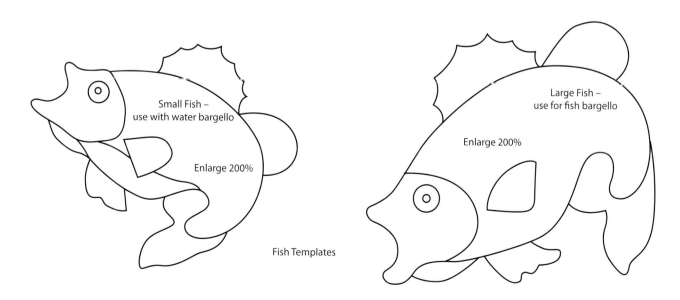

Small Fish –
use with water bargello

Enlarge 200%

Large Fish –
use for fish bargello

Enlarge 200%

Fish Templates

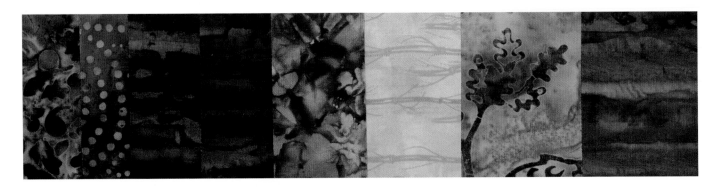

Bits of Bargello
Gallery

Quilts shown in the gallery were made or commissioned by the author.

T-Rex Sonrise

42" x 56½"
Landscape Bargello

The Entourage

60" x 21"
Reverse Appliqué Bargello

Churn Dash I

38½" x 43½"
Bargello in blocks

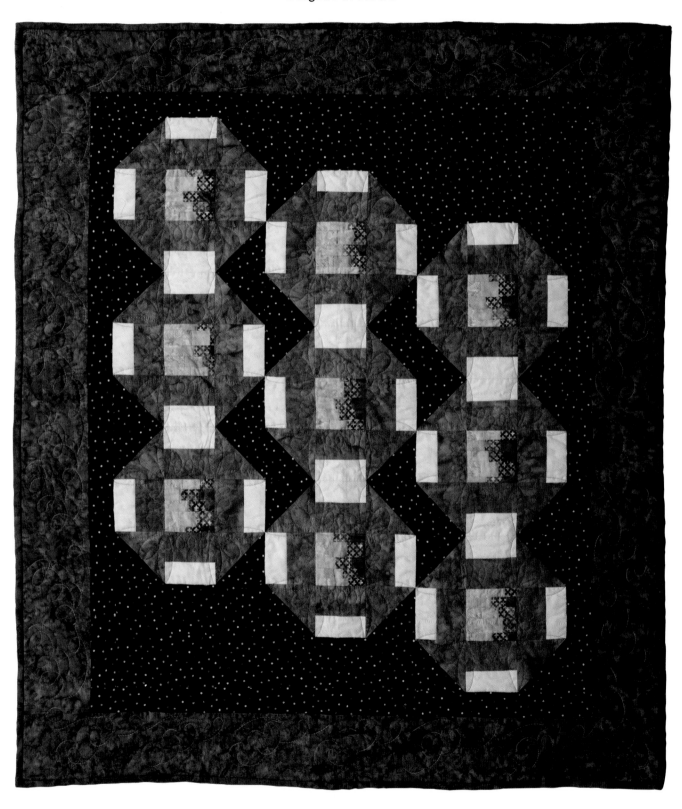

Friendship Star

52" x 62"
Bargello in blocks

Rail Fence

45" x 51½"
Bargello in blocks

Butterflies & Daisies

50" x 58"
Reverse Appliqué Bargello

Bargello Rails

27" x 27"

Bargello in blocks

Star Flower

42" x 42"
Bargello in blocks

Bargello Circles

84" x 84"
Bargello in blocks

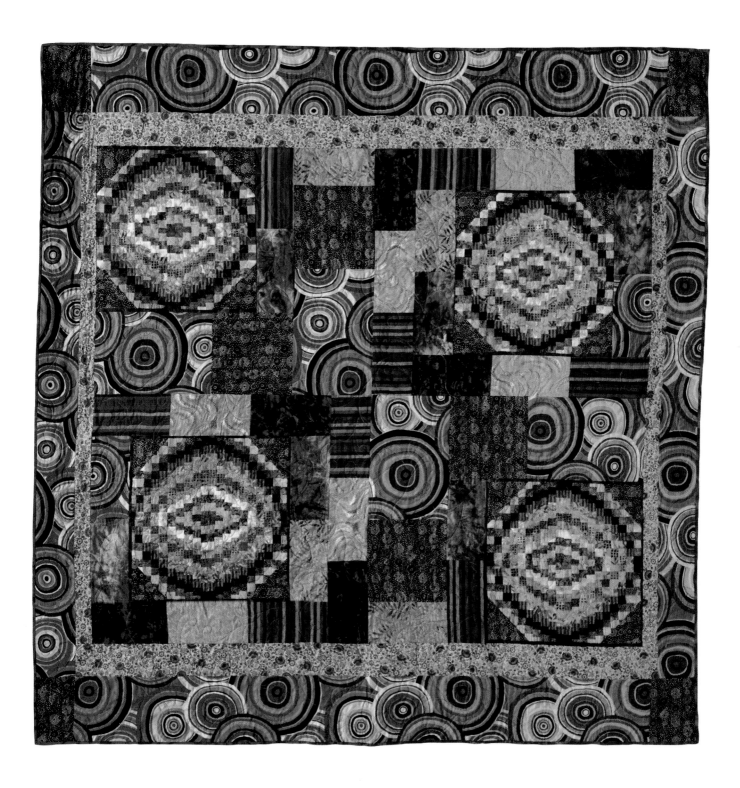

Through the Woods

72" x 74"

A combination of bargello in blocks and landscape bargello

BITS *of* Bargello – Karen Gibbs

Churn Dash II

35" x 35"
Bargello in blocks

Glossary

Straight fabric: background fabrics to which bargello bits are appliquéd or pieced

Bargello buddies: the fabrics that hang out with each other in a bargello sequence. They're built into strip sets that are cut into segments. The segments are then sewn together in a specific sequence to create a bargello unit

Bargello bit: a shape or section cut from a bargello unit to appliqué or piece into a quilt

Bargello unit: a series of strip-set segments sewn together

Bargello sequence: the arrangement of bargello buddy strip-set segments; the completed bargello from which the bargello bits are cut

Bargello segment: a pieced strip cut from a strip-set of bargello buddy fabrics

Staystitch: a straight stitch around a shape to stabilize fabric or a pieced unit prior to cutting

Resources

Cottage Mills: Creative Products for Creative People
PO Box 414
Waunakee, WI 53597
608-850-3660
800-322-1270
www.cottagemills.com
ColorScope™ Color Selector

Mary Ellen Products
Mary Ellen's Best Press spray starch is available in several scents and can be ordered unscented.
www.maryellenproducts.com

Niagara makes a non-aerosol spray starch that is available at grocery stores.

Reynolds 18" wide freezer paper comes in 75' and 150' rolls and is available at grocery and hardware stores.

Ricky Tims
Tims Art Quilt Studio and Gallery
PO Box 392
105 West Ryus Ave
La Veta, CO 81055
www.rickytims.com
Stable Stuff® Poly
8½" x 11" sheets

Plastic sheet protectors are available wherever office supplies are sold.

Quilters Treasure Marbled Fabric
Original marbled fabrics
603-532-7232
www.quilterstreasure.com

Meet the Author

Photo by Jim Pachter, Pachter Photography

Karen Gibbs is the owner/designer of The Quilt Studio, a multi-faceted design studio in Ballston Lake, New York, which includes a longarm quilting and design service and a pattern design division.

Karen has a background in textile design, previously working in the River Art division of Eagle's Eye, a clothing manufacturer in Conshohocken, Pennsylvania. Eagle's Eye was mainly known for their sweaters depicting holiday scenes with coordinating turtlenecks. Each sweater was graphed out, with designs broken down into little rectangles, each rectangle representing a stitch. During this time, Karen began teaching herself quilting, learning quickly what a rotary cutter was. Combining quilting with endless rectangles brought her to bargello.

Karen's family is a continual source of inspiration, looking at the world through her children's eyes. She is an active member of Wings Falls Quilters Guild, which (according to her husband) meets for the entire day on the second Saturday of every month!

Learn more about Karen by visiting her Web site, www.thequiltstudio.com.

For today's quilter… inspiration and creativity from

AQS Publishing

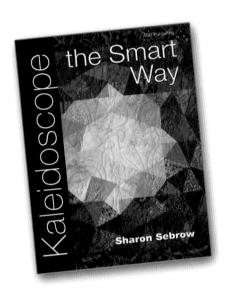

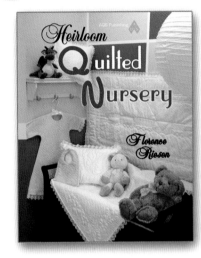

Look for these books nationally. Call or Visit our Web site at

1-800-626-5420

www.AmericanQuilter.com